THROUGH THE
HARD TIMES AND
THE GOOD

Front cover: Residents of Orme Road celebrate King George VI's coronation in 1937.
Back cover: Worthing promotes its charms in London, *c.*1950s.

To my mother, Shirley Hare, who has been there
for me 'through the hard times and the good'.

First published in the United Kingdom in 2009 by
Guild Care
Methold House,
North Street
Worthing
Sussex BN11 1DU
history@guildcare.org
www.guildcare.org

Registered charity no. 1044658

British Library Cataloguing in Publication Data
A catalogue record for this book is available from the British Library

ISBN: 978-0-9563171-0-0

Copyright text © Christopher Hare 2009

Design and production: Mike Blacker
Blacker Design
Hillcroft Barn
Coombe Hill Road
East Grinstead
West Sussex RH19 4LY
info@blackerdesign.co.uk

Printed and bound in China by 1010 Printing Ltd

THROUGH THE HARD TIMES AND THE GOOD

AN ORAL AND SOCIAL HISTORY OF WORTHING

CHRIS HARE

Acknowledgements

My deepest thanks go to all the following, who are listed in order of when they became involved in the project.

Project bid: Jane Weston

Heritage Lottery Fund: Hannah Vernon, Christine Garwood

Guild Care: Bob Phipps, Julia Johnson, Luke Knight, Claire Binstead

Steering Group: Martin Hayes, Julia Johnson, Clare Nitman, Mick Plumb, Alan Readman, Jane Weston

Archival Research: Dorothy Brooks, Roger Davies, Moyna Faulkner, Karen Foster, Kate Guy, Bill Geddes, Matthew Homewood, Anne Honniball, Oliver Holbrook, Barrie Keech, Jean Maile, Jacqueline Maina, Clare Nitman, Emma Norton, Robin Prieber, Andrea Pyle, Barbara Randall, Oliver Smith-Boyes, Jane Weston

Oral history interviews conducted by: June Fuhrmann, Craig Mackay

Scanning of old photographs: Caroline Adams and Claire Snoad

Transcription of oral history interviews: Ann Heron, Jean Maile, Andrea Pyle, Jill Startup

Highlighting of research themes within the transcriptions: Karen Foster, Barrie Keech, Barbara Randall

Editor: Ann Feloy

Proof-reading: Elwyn Blacker, Dorothy Brooks, Patrick Campbell, Anne Honniball, Barrie Keech, Craig Mackay, Jean Maile, Barbara Randall, Gill Smith-Boyes

Content advice: Martin Hayes, Jacqueline Simpson

IT Support: James Holley, Matt Holley

Other help, including searches of Ancestry.com: Chris Allen, Barrie Keech, Phillip Wood

Photographic/image acknowledgements: I would like to thank the following individuals and organisations for their permission to reproduce the photographs that appear on the following pages: Worthing Herald 7, 105; Guild Care 9, 11, 13, 15, 16, 19, 21, 36, 67, 69, 73, 74, 75, 77, 79, 81, 82, 83, 84, 85, 86, 87, 88, 89, 90, 91, 92, 93, 108, 119, 125, 126, 129, 131, 132, 147, 148, 149, 150, 151, 152, 153, 154; Mary Martin 23, 24, 25, 29, 30, 39, 41, 118; Worthing Museum (with special thanks to Gerry Connolly) 26, 27, 34, 35, 38, 40, 45, 47, 49, 50, 51, 52, 55, 56, 58, 59, 62, 63, 65, 72, 106, 115, 116, 127, 134; Cynthia Davey 28, 37, 70, 139; Barbara Knight 31; West Sussex County Council Library Service 32, 61, 136; Mary McKeown 33, 144; Denis Spells 43, 44, 46; Ann Miller 71; Bob Spanswick 95, 101, 102; Mark Fuhrmann 96; Phoebe Coombes 97; John Sams 98, 100, 113; St. Andrew's High School 103, 122, 123; Shirley Hare 109; Denise Rason 110, 128; Brian McCluskie 111, 140; Faith Pakenham Beatty 112; Wendy Greene 120, 130; Margaret Hallard, 121; Roger Davies 135; Chris Hare 137; Leigh Lawson 138; Dorothy Till 142; Gina Wilmshirst 143. Thanks also to Robin Baker for alerting me to the existence of the photographs at St Andrews School

Design/production: Blacker Design, especially Mike, Cindy, Simon and Elwyn

Indexer: John Goulding

Contents

Introduction

his book is the culmination of an ambitious, two-year process that began when Jane Weston of Worthing Carer's Support Service submitted a bid on Guild Care's behalf to the Heritage Lottery Fund (HLF) for a project to celebrate the Guild's 75th anniversary. That bid was successful and I was privileged to be appointed manager of what became known as the 'Time for History' project. Our aim was to research and record the history of Guild Care in the broader context of Worthing's social history.

At the outset, I was impressed to find Guild Care had an extensive archive of historic documents, including newspaper cuttings files going back to the 1930s, as well as all the annual reports and minute books of the various Guild Care committees. With a team of volunteers, some of whom put in many long hours of research, we worked throughout the summer and autumn of 2008, making notes from these documents, which proved invaluable in preparing the text for this book.

The initial bid envisaged oral history interviews with 30 people who could recall the events and incidents described in the archive. However, following a 'History Day' at Worthing Library in August 2008, more than 80 people came forward with their memories of growing up in the town. Those people quoted in this book were born between 1910 and 1964, with the majority being born in the 1930s and 1940s. Their reminiscences were recorded on to tape and cd and these interviews were then transcribed word for word – a long and painstaking task.

Early on in the project, I recruited a team of volunteers and ran training sessions in archival research and oral history interview techniques. At various times, some 25 people were involved, about half of whom remained active throughout the project. Furthermore, a steering group, including representatives of Guild Care, the West Sussex Record Office and the *Worthing Herald*, ensured the project stayed on track and remained true to its original objectives.

As far as possible I have sought to reference the material, whether oral or archival, in as user-friendly a way as possible, with references being listed at the end of each chapter. In a few instances, oral history respondents have asked for anonymity and, of course, this has been respected. In Chapter 4, when discussing allegations of wrong-doing, I have used a letter rather than a surname to identify the individuals concerned. This seemed the right thing to do, not just in regards to these individuals' reputations, but also in recognition of the possible hurt that could be caused to living relatives.

All the written sources are referenced in the traditional way, with a small number corresponding to a written reference at the end of each chapter. The oral history sources are not referenced in this way but in a manner I believe will be beneficial to the reader, while giving due recognition to the interviewee. Interviewee's names are referred to in the text itself, with their date of birth in square brackets, e.g. Madge Smith [b.1925],

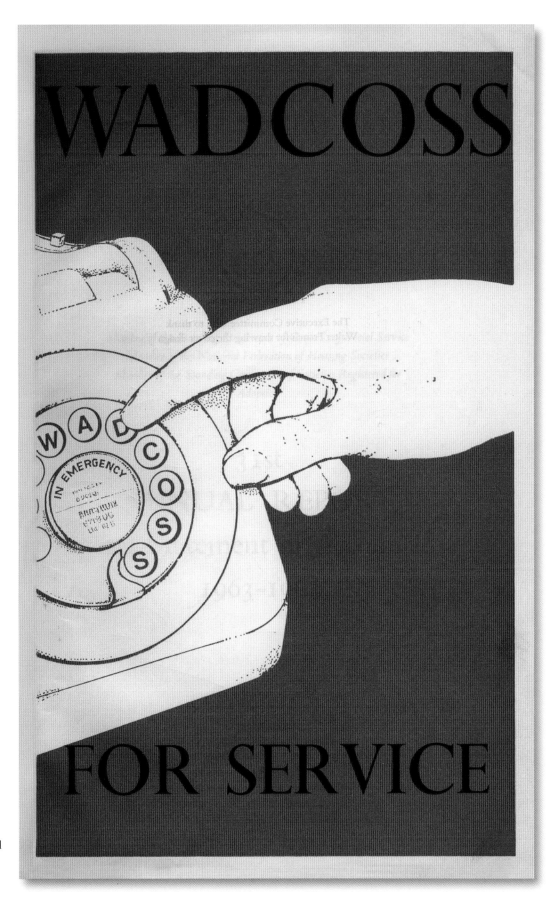

Worthing and
District Council
of Social Service
(WADCOSS) annual
report front cover,
1963/64.

thus clearly distinguishing the oral from the archival source material. The date of birth allows the reader to understand the context of the memory, i.e. whether the person was a child or an adult at the time of the event they were describing.

All those interviewed and quoted appear in an additional index to the subject index, making it easier for them, their relatives and friends to find their quotations in the book. It may also be helpful for readers wishing to identify memories of people born within a specific time frame.

Apologies must be given to those people we interviewed who do not appear in this book. Everyone had a story to tell and there was not one interview that did not reflect, in some new or special way, the history of our town. It is hoped that a further book including these memories will be published in the future.

Although the extracts from the interviews are not reproduced with every 'um' and 'ah' retained, I have sought to reproduce real speech, conveying true meaning and emotion. Very few people speak in perfect sentences without hesitation or digression, in the manner of a television newsreader – real speech, real conversation is not like that. When we interviewed people for this project, we spoke to them for between 30 and 90 minutes. This needs to be borne in mind when reading the short extracts from those interviews that appear in this book. The interviewee has spoken the words but, as in general practice, the author – the historian – in this case myself, is the one who has made the selection. All history is partial and although I have aimed to let the history and particularly the people who lived through it speak for themselves, another historian might have made different choices. I hope that the interviewees, as well as the readers of this book, will approve of the choices I have made.

The organisation today known as Guild Care has, over the course of its 76 years, been known by several names. Although the changes of name are referred to several times in the text, I think it is as well to set them out here, including the initials by which they were known:

1933–1958 – Worthing Council of Social Service (WCSS)
1958–1979 – Worthing and District Council of Social Service (WADCOSS)
1979–1995 – Worthing Area Guild for Voluntary Service (WAGVS)
1995 to present day – Guild Care (the Worthing Council of Voluntary Service was another off-shoot of WAGVS in 1995).

The evolution of the Guild is told over the following pages, but, in brief, it may be said that the organisation has moved from being a charity with a very broad remit run entirely by volunteers, to one that now specialises in the needs of older people and carers, staffed by highly trained professionals. The Guild's headquarters are at Methold

Guild Care annual review front cover, 2007/08.

annual review 2007-2008

1933-2008 **Guild Care**
seventy five years of caring

1933 - 2008

YEARS OF CARING

Working for older people and carers

House. It has four residential homes – Ashmount, Caer Gwent, Irene House, Linfield – and flatlets for independent living at Dolphin Court, as well as the Ashdown Road playgroup. Guild Care still depends, to a great extent, on its large team of dedicated volunteers to help deliver its wide range of services at the above premises, as well as running four charity shops and providing a volunteer driver service.

This has, without doubt, been the most exciting, interesting and rewarding project I have ever been involved in. I believe this book offers new and thought-provoking insights into the social history, not just of Worthing, but of society in general. The credit for this must lie with the rich source material and with the keen eyes and dedication of the volunteer researchers and interviewers who helped me in this work and made this project and this book possible. I wish to thank all those who gave so freely of their time and to such good effect. All those who helped with the research and production of this book are mentioned in the acknowledgements, and it will be seen how varied and far reaching were the skills required to enable this book to be in your hands today.

Special thanks must go to Sarah Dale and Mick Plumb at the *Worthing Herald* who gave their time and skills free of charge in order to produce the DVD that is included with this book. It is hoped the DVD will be a useful introduction to the book and that the interviews with six of the original interviewees will bring their testimony alive and perhaps inspire others to undertake similar research.

Those wishing for further or background reading on the history of Guild Care should consult the following studies, all of which are kept in the reference section at Worthing Library:

50 Years of Caring by Frank Cave, published by WAGVS in 1983 and republished with additional information in 1987.

The Guild's First Residential Home, 1943–1953 by Edward Kellett, published (as a memorial to Frank Cave) by WAGVS in 1993.

The History of Guild Care, 1933–1998, The First 65 Years by Edward Kellett, published by Guild Care in 1999.

Lastly, readers may be interested to know that all the research material for this book, including both the written and oral archives, has been transferred to the safe keeping of West Sussex Record Office at Chichester. I am very happy to advise anyone wishing to see or research the archive and can be contacted at **chrisharex@yahoo.co.uk**

Chris Hare – 'Time for History' Project Officer.
Worthing, June 2009

Television personalities Wilfred and Mabel Pickles arrive to open Methold House in 1958. This was the original Methold House at 9 North Street. The current Methold House was opened in 1975.

T oday Guild Care, which celebrated its seventy-fifth anniversary in 2008, is a highly respected Worthing-based charity with a multi-million pound budget and a national reputation for its caring services for the elderly. Its early beginnings were quite a different story, though. The limited company of today began its existence in 1933 as a pioneering voluntary organisation that sought to co-ordinate the existing charitable efforts in the town and alleviate the acute distress that many people were experiencing during the Great Depression of the 1930s. This is the story of how that organisation, the Worthing Council of Social Service (WCSS), came into being.

Since before the First World War, particularly in the more deprived areas of Britain, there had been a growing trend for men and women involved in charitable endeavours to come together to pool their resources and co-ordinate their efforts. By the 1920s these local arrangements were being supported by a national organisation, the National Council of Social Service. With a handful of paid staff and little funding, the National Council's role was to disseminate good practice and encourage the development of professional social work – a concept then in its infancy. Most of the pioneers of this movement were, rather incongruously, former army officers and clergymen. Most of the 'foot soldiers' who volunteered their time were middle class ladies, increasingly augmented by young female professionals fresh from graduating in the new science of social work.

By the onset of the Great Depression, following the stock-market crash of 1929, people in Worthing saw little in their town to warrant such 'needy' activities as those of the National Council of Social Service. Neighbouring Brighton may have established a Centre for Social Service, but surely such measures were not required here? Not that Worthing was unwilling to dig into its collective pockets to help the disadvantaged. Since 1926, Worthing had 'adopted' the stricken Welsh town of Brynmawr, which by 1928 had an unemployment rate of 84%. Local people had donated clothing and footwear to Brynmawr and contributed hundreds of pounds to build a swimming pool in the town. Sidney Walter, a Worthing magistrate and charity volunteer, declared that, 'Amongst the inhabitants [of Brynmawr], Worthing's name is honoured and loved.'[1] Some members of the Worthing Society of Friends, (Quakers), even went to live in Brynmawr to work directly with the people there.

Yet, as the seriousness of the economic crisis deepened, even apparently affluent towns on the south coast were affected by unemployment and low wages. The truth was that the poor of Worthing had always been present, being either ignored or blamed for their reduced circumstances. For the 'deserving poor' a soup kitchen had been established in Grafton Road in 1892 by the Worthing Provident and Relief

The Revd Edmund Haviland – Rector of Heene and one of the founders of the Worthing Council of Social Service. His experiences as Vicar of Selly Oak in Birmingham convinced him of the value of co-ordinating the activities of all local charities, thereby preventing duplication or, what he termed, 'over-lapping' of services.

Benefit Society. Various almshouses around the town, funded by the bequests of wealthy individuals, gave homes to the elderly poor in their final years. For the 'undeserving poor' there was the East Preston Union Workhouse – a dreaded place of committal that no poor person would enter voluntarily.

After the First World War, Worthing Town Council built the town's first council houses, with priority going to local families where the husband had fought in the war or where the wife was a widow of a fallen serviceman. There was a growing sense that more should be done to help the poorest inhabitants but the effort was often sporadic and lacking in central or local government funding. By January 1932, there were 822 unemployed people in Worthing, up from only 252 two years earlier. The government, unable to balance its books, cut unemployment benefit and halted its funding of council house building. Clearly, even in Worthing, many people of a 'deserving' nature were suffering great hardship.

Two members of the Worthing Rotary Club decided that something should be done to alleviate distress locally and that 'something' needed to be focused and adequately funded. The two men in question were the Revd E. Arthur Haviland who, the previous year, had become Rector of Heene, and Arthur Linfield of the well-known Worthing market gardening firm.

Haviland had been born at Hitchin in Hertfordshire in 1874, where his father was the rector. As a young man his father had been a curate at Herstmonceux in Sussex. The young Haviland had 12 siblings and the household employed eight servants to look after the family, so his upbringing was certainly privileged. He followed his father into the ministry and by 1909 was Vicar of Selly Oak in Birmingham, where he had four clergy assisting him and three live-in servants.[2] It was here that Haviland observed real poverty for the first time and also a co-ordinated effort by local charitable workers of the type that would inspire his activities twenty years later in Worthing.

John Sams [b.1922] recalls Haviland's time as rector at Heene, and in particular a discussion group that the rector chaired in the parish. On one occasion, the young Sams got into a heated theological discussion with an older member of the group that threatened to turn nasty but was defused by Haviland's diplomatic intervention:

I can remember Haviland being so considerate to me as a youngster, healing the breach between myself and this old buffer. He was a lovely chap. He really was.

Arthur Linfield was born in Worthing in 1885 and followed his father, also Arthur, into the family business. Linfield senior had become famous in Worthing for his charity work and in particular for his tireless activity during the typhoid epidemic of 1893, when 188 people died and over 1,400 became seriously ill. As his son, by then 'Sir' Arthur Linfield, recalled in 1974:

I remember him going around in a horse-drawn cab during that 'fever year' to cottages, carrying blankets and helping carry out patients to take them to the temporary hospital set up in Worthing High Street. He devoted a lot of his life to work for the poor and he was also a very good Christian, which set me a good example as a boy.[3]

Arthur Linfield (later 'Sir Arthur') was another of the founders of WCSS. He had been inspired to undertake charitable work by the efforts of his father in helping distressed families in Worthing during the typhoid epidemic of 1893.

Linfield senior was a town councillor who later became mayor and in the 1920s he was elected as a Liberal MP for Bedfordshire. Clearly Linfield junior was inspired by his father's example, and although he never followed him into politics, he did serve on many important local and regional bodies, becoming chairman of the health authority and of Gifford House, the home for wounded ex-servicemen. Frank Cave, editor of the *Worthing Herald* from 1932–1967 and another important player in the Guild Care story, believed that, 'by any standards', Arthur Linfield was 'a great man'.[4]

It was in April 1932, at the instigation of Haviland and Linfield, that Major Carter of the National Council of Social Service addressed a meeting of the Worthing Rotary Club to which representatives from 'other committees and associations' in the town were invited. Major Carter set out the ethos behind the National Council and the practical good that could be done at the local level. In words uncannily resembling those of

President John F. Kennedy, delivered thirty years later, Major Carter attempted to define the effect that he and his colleagues were hoping to bring about :

> *The real service of society is in trying to get people to realise their place in society; not only what society should do for them, but what they should and can do for society.*[5]

One wonders if JFK's speechwriters had access to the minute books of Worthing Rotary Club.

Although the speech was well-received, it proved a challenge to translate the initial interest in Major Carter's address into action on the ground. Other towns might need a Council of Social Service, but surely things were not really that bad here in Worthing? Haviland recalled: 'It was difficult at first to find anybody who thought it necessary.'[6]

However, both Haviland and Linfield persisted and that autumn a meeting was held at Heene Rectory to further the aim of establishing a Council of Social Service in Worthing. Momentum was given to their cause by the increasing economic gloom – even in Worthing. That Christmas the Worthing Rotary Club appealed to its members to find work for the unemployed; to look around their homes and see what they needed doing in terms of repairs and decoration.[7]

However, in March 1933, the *Worthing Herald* was reporting on a disappointing response to the 'Spend for Employment' appeal in the town – a national appeal that had been far better supported in other towns where a co-ordinated approach to fund raising had proved its worth.[8]

On the 5 April 1933, a meeting was held at Heene Parish Rooms, the purpose being to establish in Worthing a Council of Social Service. At the time Haviland was chaplain to the town's mayor, Councillor T.E. Hawkins, who had issued invitations to the meeting from the Town Hall. Writing 25 years later, Haviland recalled: 'The mayor's support was of the greatest value. It put us on the map and was, no doubt, the main reason why there was such a good attendance'.[9] Miss Mary Tudor from the Brighton Social Services Centre gave an 'admirable explanatory talk' and a resolution was passed to establish the 'Worthing Council of Social Service'. It was also agreed that the prime purpose of the new organisation would be to assist those in need but not presently receiving help, and to promote co-operation between different local organisations.

Setting up the Worthing Council of Social Service, (WCSS), was the easy part. Now it had to deliver. The new body became responsible for the Spend for Employment Fund in Worthing, now standing at £26,201, and the Worthing Unemployed Allotment Association, established by the Worthing Society of Friends (Quakers). It also hoped to fund a form of legal aid in the town and to introduce subsidised dental treatment for poorer people. There was also a new Centre for the Unemployed at the Literary Institute in Montague Street, where the men could receive refreshments and listen to lectures organised by the Worthing branch of the WEA (Workers Education Association). These were ambitious aspirations. However, WCSS lacked both permanent offices and a permanent secretary.

Hopes that Worthing Town Council would find accommodation for WCSS in the new town hall, opened that year by Prince George, were soon dashed. Offices were at last secured at 1 Colonnade House in the High Street, but within a year WCSS had to move again, this time to offices at 11 Liverpool Terrace. This, however, was a minor problem. The real difficulty lay in the inability to find a permanent secretary, or at least one who would stay on the modest salary offered. In this first eighteen months there were three temporary secretaries: Miss Scott, Miss Curtis and Miss Richards. Finally, in September 1934, a permanent position was secured by the appointment of Miss Phyllis Wood who, it was noted in WCSS's first annual report, had been 'trained for Social Work at the London School of Economics and at the Women's University Settlement, Southwark, and has worked at Brighton Social Service Centre'. The report concluded with due *gravitas* that 'the Council would like to emphasize the importance of its employing a qualified Social Worker as Secretary'.[10]

However, a year later, Miss Wood left to get married and was replaced by another well-qualified social worker, Miss Jane Robertson. Yet, in little over a year, she too would be gone to a better paid job in London. All the time, unnoticed, one of the honorary assistant secretaries, Mrs Ethel Methold, although lacking any professional qualifications, was getting a very clear idea of what needed to be done if WCSS was to be a success and achieve its aims.

Meanwhile, doubts were being raised as to how effective WCSS was proving to be in its new role. One critic, writing to the *Worthing Herald*, dismissed WCSS as being 'ineffective, parochial, clerical', suggesting that wealth distribution was preferable to charity.[11] The well-known writer and radio broadcaster S.P.B. Mais, who lived at Shoreham, lambasted efforts that provided 'facilities [for the unemployed] only to go on doing nothing'. What was needed was to provide the unemployed with real jobs.[12]

After eighteen months, the WCSS offices were open on weekday mornings, which was an improvement on the initial two mornings a week. Arthur Linfield sought to bolster flagging morale and declared that WCSS's aims could be achieved for 'a ridiculously small sum', and he pleaded to people of Worthing to, 'Back us up and I am sure it will do a lot of good to the community'.[13] Revd Haviland assured the critics that much was being done, but the details could not be stated publicly due to client confidentiality. Far from just dispensing charity, WCSS was fully enquiring into cases and seeking to provide long-term solutions to individual need.[14]

There can be little doubt – for the records prove it – that the fortunes of WCSS changed for the better the day they appointed their sixth secretary in four years. However, this secretary had no professional qualifications and no experience apart from that of being an assistant secretary. Ethel Methold, appointed to succeed Jane Robertson and known to everyone as 'Effie' Methold, (but always referred to in official minutes as 'Mrs Bernard Methold,' following the custom in those days of the wife taking her husband's full name when used in a formal sense), would implement with practical good sense the vision that had inspired Haviland and Linfield.

Within a year of taking charge, Mrs Methold had: opened the offices mornings and afternoons; established a rudimentary legal aid service; overseen the introduction of a free dentistry scheme for adolescents – the first of its type in the country; introduced the distribution of free school milk for poorer children; started a 'Boot Scheme' to provide subsidised or free footwear and was actively campaigning for Nursery Class provision in Worthing. For the first time WCSS finances were in the black.

If this was not impressive enough, the number of people seeking assistance at the WCSS offices or making enquiries on behalf of others rose from a few hundred to 3,690 in the year 1937/38. Little wonder then that WCSS's annual report for that year could conclude:

The Council has been able more fully than in any previous year to come nearer to realising the spirit and the letter of its aims.[15]

Effie Methold was to remain Honorary Secretary until her untimely death in 1957. It is not surprising that obituary notices lauded her unequalled contribution. What is more telling are the fulsome tributes and praises that were bestowed upon her throughout her career with WCSS and also those made many years after her death by those who had known her best.

Her origins had been quite humble. Both her parents had been domestic servants, although by the time of her birth in 1904, her father, Thomas Simpkins, was working as the 'Steward of Cavendish Mansions', recently opened in a fashionable district of London, (though he was probably, in reality, only a rather up-market caretaker). Effie was an only child and it is quite startling that her mother was 48 when she gave birth to her – an advanced age for a first child today – almost unheard of then. Could Effie have been adopted? It is only

Ethel 'Effie' Methold, the person who, as Honorary Secretary, steered WCSS through the Depression and war years. She was awarded an MBE in 1946 and died, aged only 53, in 1957. 'She was a great fighter who hated to admit defeat'.

speculation, but until the Adoption Act of 1927, such arrangements were nearly always informal and without official approval. It is interesting that Effie and her husband, whom she married in 1930, never had children. Bernard Methold had a successful career in the insurance industry and by 1936 the couple were living at 'Flints' – a detached and recently built house in Offington Avenue – then, as now, a very desirable address.[16] It would seem that Effie was determined to do all she could for those who had not been so lucky in life as herself, and particularly children. She was to be the driving force behind WCSS being approved as the county's only official adoption agency in 1952.

In 1953, the then chairman of WCSS, the Revd Barnard Spaull, said of Mrs Methold:

She has given service that, measured by financial standards, would certainly be beyond the capacity of the Council to repay, and has never stinted herself in giving her time, her skill and her experience in the service of the community of Worthing and district.[17]

After her death, Spaull declared:

It is true when she became Honorary Secretary that the Council began to develop into the major organisation which it has now become. Increasingly she gave it something of her own personality.[18]

Writing in 1983, Frank Cave gave his appreciation of Mrs Methold's contribution to WCSS:

She was a most remarkable person: a treasure as an administrator, compassionate, but whose kindness never overruled her sound commonsense and judgement. She was persistent in things she thought needed to be pursued and this related as much to a comparatively trifling application for financial help as it did to a policy matter . . .

. . . Effie Methold felt other people's weaknesses and needs deeply. She was a great fighter and hated to admit defeat. Many people helped secure and develop the work of the Worthing Council of Social Service but . . . she was the greatest of them all.[19]

Frank Cave himself was also central to the success of WCSS in its early days and, indeed, remained a key player right up until his death in 1992. Frank came to Worthing from Bristol as a young man to work as a reporter on a new local newspaper – the *Worthing Herald*. In 1932, aged only 25, he was appointed editor, a position he held until his retirement in 1967. It was in his capacity as editor that Frank Cave was able to give extensive coverage to the activities and campaigns of

Frank Cave became acting editor of the *Worthing Herald* in 1932 and was confirmed in the post two years later, aged only 27. He remained editor until 1967. One of the other founders of WCSS, Frank remained active in the organisation up until his death in 1992.

John Sams (on the left), former Chairman of WCSS, is seen unveiling a commemorate plaque to Frank Cave in 1993. Also present is Mary Wilton, Mayor of Worthing.

WCSS. Without his backing in 1933, WCSS might never have succeeded in establishing itself. Very soon he was working on WCSS's Personal Services Committee which decided on individual applications for help and support. He later became chairman of the committee and then chairman of the executive committee. After the death of Sir Arthur Linfield in 1974, Frank was made Life President of WCSS.

As he outlived the other three 'founders' by between 18 and 35 years, and remained active in WCSS, (or Worthing Area Guild for Voluntary Service as it was known by then), until his death, Frank Cave is still well-remembered today. These reminiscences are honest and fondly given, but include all aspects of the man's character and personality.

Brian McCluskie [b.1935] was a young reporter on the *Worthing Herald* in the 1950s and remembers Frank Cave at the height of his powers:

He was a very . . . I wouldn't say a hard task master but he believed in getting everything right, you know. He was somebody who was determined to produce the best newspaper in the country.

In 1958, the *Worthing Herald* beat off competition from national newspapers to be voted the best newspaper for design and content in the country – something rarely achieved by a local newspaper.

Arthur Linfield's daughter, Molly Cormick [b.1917] remembers that 'he was great fun'. Ron Duddy [b.1926], who worked with Frank in the 1970s and 80s at WCSS and later the Guild, recalls him as 'a wonderful character – a stickler for tradition'. Lillian Holdsworth [b.1937], who as Lillian Phillips was chairman of the Guild in the 1980s, remembers that 'Frank was tremendously hard-working and had a heart of gold.' However, she also conceded that he could 'rub people up the wrong way'. Indeed, John Sams [b.1922], who held many positions with WCSS over the years, including that of chairman of the council, stated that 'Frank Cave was the most difficult man I ever met,' but added, 'Yet by his determination things were kept going, perhaps that might not have, which might have collapsed through lack of effort.'

Kay McLoughlin, who was chairman of the executive committee in the 1970s, remembers someone who 'was absolutely dedicated to the Guild, but [who] was a difficult man. He didn't suffer fools gladly . . . but it was all for the love of the Guild.' Alan Desmond [b.1927], a long-time WCSS and Guild volunteer, recalls how, even in his eighties, Frank Cave would be found helping with the gardening in the Guild's care homes. Indeed, shortly before his death, he was working in the pouring rain in one such garden. He would also regularly take his meals with the residents at Dolphin Court. As Alan says, 'The Guild was his life.'

Together these four extraordinary people – Haviland, Linfield, Methold and Cave – charted a new direction in the social history of Worthing, and one that this book seeks to trace from the 1930s to the present day.

References

1　*Worthing Herald*, 16 July 1932

2　Research undertaken on the internet by Chris Allen. (www.ancestry.co.uk)

3　*West Sussex Gazette*, 24 January 1974

4　Cave, Frank, *50 Years of Caring*, (Worthing Area Guild for Voluntary Service, 1983 & 1987)

5　*Worthing Herald*, 9 April 1932

6　WCSS Annual Report, 1957/58

7　*Worthing Herald*, 24 December 1932

8　*Worthing Herald*, 25 February 1933

9　WCSS Annual Report, 1957/58

10　WCSS Annual Report, 1933/34

11　*Worthing Herald*, 30 December 1933

12　*Worthing Gazette*, 21 March 1934

13　*Worthing Gazette*, 24 October 1934

14　*Worthing Gazette*, 21 March 1934

15　WCSS Annual Report, 1937/38

16　Research undertaken on the internet by Barrie Keech. (www.ancestry.co.uk)

17　WCSS Annual Report, 1952/53

18　WCSS Annual Report, 1956/57

19　Cave, Frank, *50 Years of Caring*, (Worthing Area Guild for Voluntary Service, 1983 & 1987), p.16

This photograph is actually from the 1920s rather than the 30s, but it was far too good not to include. Mary Martin, who donated it, was not sure where the men were working, but they appear to be on the shingle beach. It is possible that they were repairing what was known as 'faggot walk', the coastal footpath at East Worthing. The name derived from the fact that piles of faggots were driven into the ground before a hard surface was applied. The men in the picture certainly seem to have bundles of faggots, so they may have been working on the reconstruction of the walk way.

CHAPTER 2
The Great Depression

The Great Depression of the 1930s conjures up images of massed ranks of unemployed men standing on street corners; of the hunger marches, most memorably the 'Jarrow Crusade' and of Oswald Mosley's fascist blackshirts battling with their opponents in the East End of London. Surely, genteel Worthing on the sunny south coast was not a part of this grim story? Worthing never experienced the acute hardship and suffering seen in South Wales, the north of England, or indeed parts of London, yet it is a surprise to discover just how difficult life became for many local people in the Depression years.

Unemployment, always seen as a seasonal, rather than a long-term problem in Worthing, became far more serious in the town during the 1930s. As shown in the

Workmen taking a rest from laying new pipework in Montague Street, again from the 1920s.

last chapter, there were 822 people registered as unemployed in Worthing in January 1932, a figure that did not include those too proud to register or those struggling on low-paid and part-time wages. While unemployment eased during the mid-1930s, it returned with a vengeance during the winter of 1937/38, standing at 1,193 in January 1938[1], and remaining high right through the following winter. So seriously did the Worthing Council of Social Service, (WCSS), take this deepening crisis that in 1939 they opened a soup kitchen in the town, providing over 1,000 meals for children from poor families.[2]

Worthing may not have seen hunger marches, but it was reported at one meeting of WCSS' Personal Service Committee in 1939 that a local family was 'starving'.[3] In

No. 2 New Street, where Mary Martin was born and grew up. In the doorway Mary can be seen with her aunt, Esther Walker.

These athletic young women playing bowls at Marine Gardens in the 1930s suggest that life was not hard for everyone in the Depression years.

March 1939 a bitter controversy broke out when a split occurred within the Worthing branch of the National Unemployed Workers' Movement, prompting a small breakaway faction accusing the leadership of being communists. The leadership, in its turn, denounced the dissidents as blacklegs who had actually been 'purged' from the branch.[4] This story was front-page news in Worthing at the time.

The British Union of Fascists had a strong presence in Worthing, with one of their members, Captain Budd, being an elected town councillor. Oswald Mosley himself addressed meetings in Worthing and on one occasion, in October 1934, there were running street fights between the blackshirts and their opponents following a Fascist rally at the Pier Pavilion. One local newspaper thought that the scenes witnessed that night were reminiscent of 'revolutionary Spain'[5] – an exaggeration, no doubt, but one that reflected the passions that politics aroused in ordinary people at that time.

Throughout these difficult years, WCSS was at the forefront of providing relief for those families suffering from the impact of the Depression. Not only did they provide assistance, they also introduced a number of ground-breaking initiatives designed to give poorer people the chance to help themselves. Behind all this good work was the tireless figure of Effie Methold, who seems never to have stopped or even paused as she sought to cajole, persuade and entreat councillors, solicitors, doctors and dentists to all do their bit to ensure that the services people needed were provided at a cost they could afford – which often meant no cost at all. It is striking, looking through the archives for this period, how little financial help WCSS received from either the town

Another photograph from Marine Gardens, showing a stylish group of middle class women sporting the latest fashions. The woman standing appears to be wearing the uniform of Oswald Mosley's British Union of Fascists, which had a thriving branch in Worthing during the mid-1930s – or was she just indulging in fascist chic?

or the county council and how much they depended on the goodwill and financial backing of the public.

It is worth considering what would have happened in Worthing in the 1930s to the poor and the destitute without the presence of the Worthing Council of Social Service. Throughout these years, the Personal Service Committee took on the task of helping hundreds of people who had fallen on hard times and for whom the government-funded Public Assistance programme could provide no relief. Mrs Bell, the wife of the Bishop of Chichester, believed that it was this public compassion for the poor, 'this personal touch, almost unknown in other countries', that kept Britain from 'suffering the shocks of Communism or Fascism' then being experienced across Europe.[6]

A photograph from the 1920s shows Wilfred Dell (driving), with his son, Wally, in the back. The truck looks a very 'Heath Robinson' affair, possibly cobbled together from the remnants of former army vehicles.

In its annual report of 1938, WCSS reported that it had, 'among its applicants many struggling to make ends meet, whose small income leaves no margin at all for clothes'.[7] That year, 'through the generosity' of the public, WCSS was able to find clothing for 122 Worthing families who would otherwise have gone without. The following year's report suggested that some families were no longer even able to properly feed themselves, 'People living on very small incomes, such as many in Worthing have, cannot afford food of the nutritional value necessary for good health.'[8] Such extremes of deprivation are still remembered today by the town's older residents.

Anne Buckwell [b.1913] recalls how her family bought their clothes from jumble sales and how the children's clothes were 'cut down' from men's trousers and women's dresses. Madge Aldridge [b.1920], who lived at 'bungalow town' – then a ramshackle shanty town – recalls the desperate lengths that some families would go to feed themselves. She remembers that many families ate dripping, sold very cheaply by a local family, who were themselves desperately poor. It was that very desperation that led the father of the family to tramp up to the regular army camp, held on the Downs at that time, scavenging for food:

The customers of the New Street Inn (also known as Pacey's Bloodhole). Given the blurred quality of the image, it is to be wondered if the photographer had perhaps had one beer too many?

. . . the father went up to the hill beyond Shoreham to the camp. There was a camp up there, and they used to throw out all the fat they didn't want, cut the fat off the meat and all the rest of it and this man, because the family were so poor and there was no money – there was no family allowance then – he used to go up on the hill and collect all this fat, bring it home and have great big galvanised baths on the top of the gas cooker. [the family would] boil it and boil it and then [when it had set] go round . . . he went round the beach selling dripping. People bought it [and] they were thankful to have it, 'cause times was very, very bad.

The minute books of WCSS' Personal Services Committee, taken with the annual reports, build up an intimate picture of how the council battled against the rising tide of deprivation in the 1930s. Although WCSS' funds increased year-on-year, due to fund-raising events and also to WCSS' 'subscribers' who promised to give a set amount every year, the social problems in the town increased at an even greater pace. It seemed in the winter of 1938/39 as if the WCSS would not be able to raise the funds it needed to finance all the projects to which it was committed for the benefit of 'our less fortunate brothers and sisters, and the community at large'.

It was the 'generous action of one subscriber' who did not want their name made public, that saved the day. This person promised to increase their annual subscription five-fold if 75 other subscribers would agree to double theirs. The 1938 annual report recorded that, 'the requisite number soon responded to the challenge', and so a crisis in WCSS' finances was avoided.[9] To this unnamed subscriber, WCSS tendered its gratitude and many people were clothed and fed that year as a consequence of one selfless act.

South Down Motor Services charabanc ride, a popular form of excursion between the wars.

The Personal Service Committee was able to intervene to improve the lives of hundreds of individuals and families. At all times, the committee sought to change people's lives for the long term rather than provide short term palliatives, or as WCSS' Chairman Revd Haviland put it, 'The object of our society is not to provide relief temporarily but to provide a plan by which people who come to us will be able to put themselves beyond the need of relief of any kind.'[10]

Many of those who approached WCSS found themselves ineligible, for whatever reason, to claim those state benefits that then existed. One man suffering from TB, who was able to work in the summer, suffered from long periods of illness in the winter when he was unable to work. On attempting to claim Sickness Benefit, he was told that he had been previously employed in 'non-insurable work' and was therefore not entitled to benefit, unless he first paid his National Insurance arrears – something he was unable to do. Fortunately, the Personal Services Committee looked into his case and agreed to pay the arrears, with the result that the man was then able to claim Sickness Benefit.[11] In another case, a family crippled by debt, owing arrears in both rent and rates, were given a grant by WCSS, which also found them two lodgers so that the debt would not build up again in the future.[12] Then there was the woman whose husband had been sent to prison. She was expecting another child and was worried how she would cope financially when she could no longer work. She had already placed her existing child with a foster-mother so that she could find employment. WCSS stepped in to provide her with a weekly grant until she was able

Worthing tomato growers at Highfield Nursery between the wars (now the site of West Tarring Middle School). Although they look like apples, the fruits in the baskets are actually the traditional 'love apple' tomato.

to return to work after the birth of her second child. It was hoped that, on his release from prison, the husband would again find employment.[13]

There is frequent reference in the minute books and reports to what are called 'letters', such as 'surgical letters' or 'ambulance letters', which appear to have been commitments made by subscribers to undertake the cost of these services in cases where WCSS felt there was a proven need. The following case study, taken from the WCSS archive, illustrates to use of these 'letters'. It also highlights how WCSS sought to help those who slipped through the net of the existing, limited, state welfare provisions:

> *A man, working on his own account and doing very well, was stricken with an illness and his savings were soon absorbed. His family was given an allowance by the Public Assistance Committee, and, in addition, his father, who lived with him, had the old age pension. They were just able to manage but could not continue to stay in the house as the rent was fairly high. The doctor was anxious for the man to go to a London hospital for special treatment and the Council was able to supply a number of ambulance letters to help with the cost of the transport. His wife, when relieved of the nursing of her husband, quickly found a cheaper home, and a grant was made for the removal of the furniture.*[14]

The case notes from this period also reveal how WCSS was able to help with expenses, which could make a huge difference to the long term prospects of family members. For example, there are instances of children from poor families being awarded scholarship places at grammar schools. However, the parents were unable to afford the cost of buying the school uniform. When this expense was met by WCSS, it not only alleviated the financial worry of the parents, it also provided a wonderful opportunity for the children to improve their prospects.

Unemployed men who found work in other towns, often had the problem of being unable to afford the removal of their families and possessions, so WCSS would meet the cost, either as a loan or a grant, depending on circumstance. There was also the 'Boot Scheme', started in 1938, whereby WCSS, probably in the person of Mrs Methold, had persuaded shoe shops in Worthing to donate shoes and boots to the poor.[15] Some unemployed people were unable to search for work as diligently as they might because their boots or shoes had worn out and they could not afford to buy a new pair. Children from these families might not be able to go to school for the same reason. It is sobering to realise just how lacking in the basic amenities of life such people were in the 1930s.

As already mentioned, a 'soup kitchen' was established in Worthing during the bitterly cold winter of 1938/39, when unemployment reached new record levels. In early January 1939, Blanche Fair from the Brighton Soup Kitchen came to Worthing to advise her colleagues at WCSS on how to organise and run a similar operation in the town.[16] Before the month was out, Mrs Methold and her colleagues were running

King George V's Silver Jubilee celebrations in Worthing in 1935. People interviewed for this book remembered that each school had to design a float to represent one of the dominions or colonies of the empire.

Silver Jubilee. Worthing.

These photographs show the residents of Orme Road enjoying a street party to mark the coronation of King George VI. Despite the happy occasion there is a dour quality about these pictures, reflecting the hard times that working class people were then experiencing.

Portland Road riding stables c.1930. Phoebe Coombs lived close to the stables and remembers the riders passing up the street. It is unlikely that the residents of Portland Road at that time would have been able to afford riding lessons.

a soup kitchen from Worthing Boys' Club, then in Ivy Arch Road. The meal provided was actually a 'thick, nourishing stew' rather than a soup.[17] The kitchen was open to the children of the unemployed and the poor, admission was by ticket. These tickets were distributed by the clergy and via the local schools. As well as the stew, the free meal also included a slice of bread and a cake or piece of fruit.

Although 1,084 meals were dispensed from the end of January until the end of March, some wondered why there had not been a greater take-up, given the deprivation that was known to exist in the town. Following a visit to the 'soup kitchen', Silina Fielden, writing in the *Worthing Gazette*, asked why there were not more children in attendance and believed it was because, 'The poor families of Worthing are diffident about showing their poverty', which she believed was a matter of pride for many of them – something 'hard to overcome.'[18] This theme was taken up in May by Miss Nicholls, the headmistress of Holy Trinity School, who observed, 'I think some parents rather object to it because it savours of charity. I think it would be better if it were called "canteen" instead of "soup kitchen".'[19] Mrs Methold took note, announcing that for the following winter the name would be changed to *canteen*.

If adults understood the nature of poverty, then children could be excused for not always fully appreciating the seriousness of the situation. Phoebe Coombs [b.1923], although born to poor parents, was, by the 1930s, living a better life than many of her neighbours thanks to her father's successful career as a car salesman. She recalls how the hardships experienced by a neighbouring family, appeared little more than a game to her at the time:

> I don't think we should have been in a council house. We did have enough money not to have a council house really. Mum used to make them bread puddings. A lot of people didn't used to have food. When I think of it, a girl one door away, she used to go and get stale cakes and stale buns because they were cheap – used to go down to the bakers and I was so upset my mother wouldn't let me go. She said, 'But we don't need cakes and buns,' but [I said], 'they have a lovely time – they play hopscotch in the Arcade.' And one day this girl – I could only have been about ten – got my mother's prop and she knocked the back bedroom window and I crept down and I got on my bike and I went with her. I thought it was wonderful.

Phoebe added that she did not realise at the time that her friend did not go to get the bread and cakes for fun, but out of mere necessity, it being food they needed to 'keep them going'. Phoebe's mother was appalled when she found out and made her give the cakes back. 'It never occurred to me we were luckier than other children,' she remembers.

During the Depression years, WCSS sought to ensure that at Christmas every poor family received a good festive meal and that the children received presents. The

An untitled photograph from the collection at Worthing Museum. A middle class mother and her children relax on Worthing beach during the 1930s. Notice the bathing machines in the background and the sand canoes in the foreground.

delivery of these gifts was organised by the Worthing Rotary Club, many of whose members were leading lights in WCSS. Christmas 1938 was a particularly hard one, with more families than usual being deemed deserving of Christmas charity. Earl Winterton, the town's MP, promised to give £5 to each of Worthing's charities working for the poor at Christmas, in the expectation that his example might 'stimulate others in Worthing to follow my example.'[20] Although that winter saw unprecedented charitable giving from the Worthing public, not everyone felt so pleased at the outcome. Sir Arthur Newsholme, the retired Medical Officer to the Local Government Board who had been elected as President of WCSS in 1935, pondered, in December 1938, on the real meaning of hundreds of local families relying on charity at Christmas, 'If we are proud to think that no family in Worthing will go without a good Christmas dinner, I think we should be a little ashamed that there are so many people in Worthing who are still unable to provide a dinner for themselves.'[21]

Sir Arthur Newsholme, the first President of Worthing Council of Social Service.

Some people looked to neither Public Assistance nor WCSS for relief but instead put their faith in the 'slate club'. These were savings schemes, usually run by the local pub, where the regulars put aside a small sum every week. At the end of each year the principle sum would be paid out to cover the costs of Christmas. The interest earned over the year – and preceding years – would go into a different fund, which would pay out in time of sickness. These institutions, also known as 'tontine' clubs, were very popular. Fred Avenell [b.1912], who helped his father run the *Rose and Crown* in Worthing during the 1930s, remembered that some people would save with the club who were not pub-goers, but who saw it as the easiest means of putting money aside for a 'rainy day'.

Fred's father had been forced to lay-off his two paid staff because of the effects of the Depression and instead called on his son to help out. Fred remembers his father telling him to come and work for him and that he had 'no choice' in the matter. Working in the pub, Fred observed the impact of hard times on the clientele, some of whom sought to drown their sorrows in drink. He particularly recalls 'a very unhappy man', forced through necessity to take work on the market gardens at Goring, who would walk, come rain or shine, from Goring to the *Rose and Crown*, drink two or three pints and then walk home again.

Some of the regulars were famous for the amount of alcohol they could consume. One man, 'Hambone' Reed, a fisherman and day labourer, would drink ten pints of beer every night. One week, for a bet, he agreed to drink only lemonade, and so for seven nights drank ten pints of lemonade instead of his usual beer. However, the only really aggressive drunkenness he remembered was that of some Irish labourers who often

Mary Dell (right) with her parents, Alfred and Sarah Dell.

'fought amongst themselves', but would turn on the landlord if 'you used the words, "you've had enough – you can't have any more," and then you had to be careful.'

The Depression forced large numbers of people to leave areas where unemployment was very high and seek work in regions where work was more plentiful. Many of these men and women came to Worthing, foremost amongst whom were unemployed miners from South Wales, but also included men from Ireland and the north-east of England. Both the parents of David O'Brien [b.1939] came to Worthing looking for work – his mother from Wales and his father from Ireland:

> *He was 17 when he came over, and I think one of his sisters was here first – that's why he came to Worthing, and he worked on Worthing golf course when they were building Worthing golf course. My mum, her and her friend left Wales when they were 15, I think, and went to work in Eastbourne in a hotel, or something, and why she came to Worthing I don't know, but she ended up in Worthing at the Warren School and that's how they met. She was a domestic and my dad was a butler there then.*

Many of the Welsh people coming to Worthing were pitifully poor and often very young. The following newspaper report highlights these details. It also shows how the authorities in Worthing, including WCSS, responded:

> *When, a fortnight ago, a boy of fifteen wandered into Worthing weary, hungry, and footsore – the end of a long trek from South Wales – he found friends among members of the Worthing Police Force. They put him into the care of the Probation Officer, Mr William Elphick. Without father or mother, without relations to look after him, the boy was alone in the world. His clothing was almost in rags; he had never had a job. Mrs Methold, honorary secretary of Worthing Council of Social Service, found the boy a few clothes, Mr Elphick got him work, and he is making good. But he needs more clothing for at the moment he has no complete change. His suit, too, is old. Will a Worthing woman with a boy of her own send some clothing to Mrs Methold for this boy? He is rather small for his age – fifteen – thin as a result of prolonged*

undernourishment, and needs a suit, underclothes, socks, shoes (size seven), pyjamas, handkerchiefs and a mackintosh and overcoat. Gifts should go to Mrs Methold at the offices of Worthing Council of Social Service.[22]

While some people extended a helping hand to these refugees from economic distress, others viewed the newcomers with suspicion and alarm. The writer and broadcaster, S.P.B. Mais, already referred to in chapter 1 as being a critic of WCSS, fed these anxieties about 'strangers', particularly when he quoted an unnamed local source telling him that 'life's been impossible for decent folk around Worthing' since the Welsh had arrived. The source then went on to allege that the Welsh got 'fighting drunk' in the pubs and then smashed 'every glass and bottle in the place'. Furthermore, they were accused of robbing local orchards and being sexual predators so that 'roads isn't safe at night for girls.'[23] Mais was read very widely and his views would have certainly influenced opinion in both Worthing and further afield.

A beach scene at Worthing between the wars. Note the old-style push chair in the foreground, and the fact that most people are fully clothed, despite it appearing to be a warm summer's day. The presence of the pier pavilion dates this picture to 1926 or later.

An enlarged section of this photograph appears on page 23. If these men are working on faggot walk they would have had a great deal of work to do, as the footpath was constantly being eroded by the sea.

Not everyone shared this negative perception. John Sams [b.1922] remembers working with men from Wales in the Worthing market gardens during his summer holidays, without any problems. The father of Denis Spells [b.1931] employed a Welsh man to drive his delivery lorry, again with no complaints. Derek Walker [b.1919] remembers that his parents warned him against the Welsh and that 'there was a prejudice against them'. Yet Derek saw none of this supposed aggressive behaviour, but rather remembers groups of men singing Welsh songs, sometimes as a means of raising money. He does remember that they went around in groups, but this he believes was to protect themselves from others, rather than with the intention of being intimidating.

Bob Copper [b.1915], a policeman in Worthing at this time, recalled the grinding poverty that these new arrivals to the town had experienced, and that, as is often the case, the behaviour of a minority could be ascribed to the whole. It was often the experience of poverty that led to outbreaks of violence:

> *Some of them were bloody good blokes, but some of them were a pretty rough lot, no doubt about it. I've seen them scrap over – they used to play pontoon and that in the lunch break and that – see them really, really scrap – bare knuckle, you know, blood all over the place, really laying into each other over half a crown or something like that.*

Bob also recalled how many Welsh lads married local girls and became fully integrated into the life of the community. Taken as a whole, it has to be said that those arriving in Worthing seeking work were well received, whatever part of the country they came from. However, groups of unfamiliar men, often looking the worse for wear, could generate anxiety. It needs to be remembered that only fifty years earlier people from London were regarded as 'foreigners' – an attitude that was still apparent when thousands of East End evacuees arrived in Worthing during the autumn of 1939. The following recollection of Agnes Carter [b.1916], tells as much about poorly-lit roads and semi-rural locations as it does about perceptions of the itinerant underclass:

Marine Parade and the Dome cinema. Note the absence of motor traffic and litter!

I used to cycle from Lancing College Farm to Littlehampton at that time, 'cause that's where my mother lived, and on the way back one night on my bicycle – and we only had those carbine lamps – these three tramps came out from Goring Hall – where they used to make their way as far as there and stay the night there and then go to East Preston [workhouse] the next day.... These three tramps came out and tried to stop me on my bike,[but] I managed to weave amongst them and I flew up that hill to Littlehampton non-stop, and every week when I went to my mother's I used to get tense frighten [sic] there....

Another group that received a mixed reception in Worthing were the people of the north-east, particularly those coming from Gateshead. Revd Haviland, Chairman of WCSS, was friendly with Canon H.S. Stephenson of Gateshead, who informed Haviland of the terrible conditions prevailing in that town – far worse than anything experienced in Worthing. Haviland decided that WCSS had a Christian duty to help their brothers and sisters in Gateshead and organised schemes to provide temporary employment for the young people of that town in Worthing. In 1936 he organised for 50 unemployed 'boys' from Gateshead to work as caddies on West Sussex golf courses.[24] At other times 'holiday' projects were organised for the youth of Gateshead, including sporting competitions with Worthing teams. Young women from Durham were also included in this good work.[25]

However, one of WCSS' staunchest supporters, who had assisted with generous financial donations, queried whether it was right to put so much effort into alleviating distress elsewhere when there was so much to do in Worthing. In a letter to the *Worthing Herald*, A.J. Barrett criticised Alderman Barber, Worthing's mayor, for calling on the people of the town to give generously to an appeal in aid of the people of Gateshead, while he had refused a plea for help from a local woman, 'Just a few days ago a poor woman with seven young children was ejected from a Worthing Council house, on a pouring wet day, and had everything put in the road; two days before this she wrote to the mayor of Worthing and received a reply

Mary Fox, then working as a nanny, is seen with a child in its pushchair in South Street in 1930. She had come down from Durham a year earlier in search of work, and later married and settled in the town.

informing her he could do nothing.' Helping the poor of Worthing was 'our first duty', insisted Barrett, 'then Gateshead after'.[26] Frank Cave, in his capacity as editor of the *Worthing Herald*, felt it necessary to reply to this criticism of both Barber (Worthing's only Labour mayor) and WCSS, stating that 'Worthing ought to be able to support both these good works.'

Another group of outsiders came from even further afield than Wales or Gateshead – the Basques, fleeing from the horrors of the Spanish Civil War. Once again, WCSS rose to the challenge of befriending and helping those who could no longer easily fend for themselves. Under the auspices of the International Friendship League (IFL), Beach House became a reception centre for Basque children, many of whom had either been separated from their parents, or whose parents had been killed in the shelling and bombing. As will be seen in the chapter on Health, WCSS led the way in the 1930s in providing dental care for the young and those on low incomes. When the warden at Beach House reported that many of the Basque children were in need of 'immediate' dental treatment, Mr Peckover from WCSS Dental Section was sent to assess the situation.[27] Seven Worthing dentists agreed to treat the children, and over the following months, 32 Basque children were treated,[28] the expense being borne by WCSS.

Shirley Hare [b.1930], came with her father, (who was on the ILF committee at Horsham), to visit Beach House during the summer of 1937. She remembers that 'there was a little girl with a very badly burned leg', that the children's toys – donated by local people – had been 'laid out beautifully' and didn't look as if they had been played with at all. Perhaps the children had wanted to impress their visitors, or perhaps they were too traumatised by their recent experiences to be able to play as other children did. The suffering of the Basques at the hands of Franco and his allies, Hitler and Mussolini, had given Worthing a taste of modern warfare, something they would soon experience at first hand in the Second World War, then only two years away.

As we shall see in the next chapter, it was the outbreak of world war that finally broke the stranglehold of the Great Depression, not only in Worthing but across the country though, of course, at a terrible price. Writing in 1983, Frank Cave perceived that only people of his own generation could remember how bad things had been in the 1930s. Recalling that period he declared, 'It is well to remember, and for those not then born, to be told.' It is indeed something of a revelation for the historian to research this period in Worthing's history, and important, as Frank said, that the story of those times should be told.

References

1. *Worthing Herald*, 15 January 1938
2. WCSS, Annual Report, 1938/39, p.6
3. WCSS, Personal Service Committee Minute book, 4 December 1939
4. *Worthing Herald*, 10 March 1939
5. *Worthing Herald*, 13 October 1934
6. *Worthing Herald*, 8 December 1937
7. WCSS, Annual Report, 1937/38, p.15
8. WCSS, Annual Report, 1938/39, p.6
9. WCSS, Annual Report, 1937/38, p.15
10. *Worthing Herald*, 18 December 1938
11. WCSS, Annual Report, 1935/36, p.6
12. Ibid, p.7
13. WCSS, Annual Report, 1936/37, p.11
14. Ibid.
15. WCSS, Annual Report, 1937/38, p.13
16. *Worthing Herald*, 6 January 1939
17. *Worthing Gazette*, 25 January 1939
18. *Worthing Gazette*, 3 February 1939
19. *Worthing Herald*, 12 May 1939
20. *Worthing Gazette*, 7 December 1938
21. *Worthing Herald*, 16 December 1938
22. *Worthing Herald*, 10 July 1937
23. Mais, S.P.B., *England's Character* (Hutchinson & Co. 1936), p.306
24. *The Times*, 15 October 1936
25. WCSS, Annual Report, 1934/35, p.6
26. WCSS, Personal Services Committee minute book, 31 May 1937
27. WCSS, Dental Section Committee minute book, 24 April 1937
28. WCSS, Dental Section Committee minute book, 1 November 1937

Spell's greengrocery stall by Holder's Corner, Montague Street, during the Second World War. Photographing ration queues was strictly forbidden during the war, so this type of shot is a rarity. Although the long queues were wearisome, rationing ensured a good diet and contributed to rising standards of health and well-being.

CHAPTER 3

Wartime Worthing

The Second World War brought many sorrows to Worthing, just as it did to other towns around the country. Servicemen and women were killed in action, and civilians were killed in air raids on the town; in fact, 44 Worthing people were killed by enemy attacks and a further 216 wounded or injured.[1] Yet despite the horrors of war, there was, albeit at great cost, an aspect to the hostilities that proved very beneficial – the Great Depression was finally brought to an end.

Initially, WCSS viewed the declaration of war on 3 September 1939 as yet another burden that it would have to carry, on top of the great weight of social deprivation it was already trying to tackle. The annual report published at the close of 1940 reported that the year just ended had been the most demanding in WCSS' seven-year history, with a record number of people requesting help or assistance. It was recorded that 827 telephone calls had been received and that 5,849 people had attended the offices in Liverpool Terrace, nearly 2,000 more than in the previous year.[2]

However, twelve months later the situation was transformed. The annual report for 1941 concluded that, 'It is fair to say that the degree of distress in the town is not as great as has, unfortunately, had to be recorded in previous reports.'[3] The following

The aftermath of a bombing raid on a warehouse in Chatsworth Road. The building was restored and is today used as a nightclub and bar.

Worthing Pier, with a hole blown in the middle – a defensive measure against it been used as a landing stage by invading forces.

year a further improvement was recorded, it being noted that, for the first time, no call had been made on either WCSS' Loan or 'Spend for Employment' Funds.[4] The same year a headline in the *Worthing Herald* declared that 'War has solved town's unemployment problem.'[5] Something remarkable had taken place in the space of two years; the war had created a wholly new approach to society and social inequality.

It is a general impression that a fairer, more just society was ushered in by the Labour victory in the general election of 1945, which led to the introduction of the National Health Service and the Welfare State. While this is true to a considerable degree, the important reforms of the 1940–45 Churchill Coalition Government are often over-looked. The high level of unemployment, poverty and low wages alluded to in the last chapter, had already receded in Worthing by 1942, three years before Attlee's famous election triumph.

The minute books and annual reports of WCSS highlight three major changes that had taken place in Worthing between 1940 and 1942, two of them legislative and one of them cultural. The Supplementary Old Age Pension, introduced in 1940, gave extra payments to those experiencing real hardship. In Worthing the result was that 'scores of old people' who would have sought relief from WCSS' Personal Service Fund were now able to pay their expenses, such as heating and rent, which previously they could not have afforded.

Firemen in the bomb-
damaged building in
Chatsworth Road enjoy a
well-deserved hot drink.

Likewise, the Dependants' Supplementary Service Allowance gave wives and mothers a weekly income from state funds to ensure that they could provide for the needs of themselves and their children while their husbands were serving in the Armed Forces. This new benefit had a huge effect in reducing poverty levels across the country.

The cultural change partly followed as a result of these administrative changes, but also as a consequence of the war creating a greater sense of there being 'one people', united against a common enemy. It was no longer as acceptable, as it had once been, to promulgate social distinctions and with it the toleration of low wages and high rents. WCSS noted 'an increase in employment and the payment of higher wages'.[6] WCSS Honorary Solicitor Robert Cushing took up the cases of those tenants deemed to be paying too high a rent and, on one occasion, secured, not just a lower rent, but a substantial rebate on rent already paid.[7] In the early years of the war, WCSS was also able to finance the removal of the unemployed to other parts of the country where workers were needed in the munitions industry.[8]

Back in the 1930s, some of those dentists working on the WCSS Dental Scheme to

An emergency reservoir in Findon Valley. Present-day Findon Valley Library stands close to the site.

provide subsidised dentistry for the poor had insisted that they would not treat those of too inferior a social class. Such attitudes were now far less tolerated. Molly Cormick [b.1917], the daughter of Arthur Linfield, believed that the war helped end the old social system whereby 'classes lived separately,' and that this loosening of class divisions was 'the one thing' that the war did 'that was good'.

If there was a social downside to the war – apart from the obvious toll of casualties in the fighting – the losers were among the professional middle class. The father of Janet Runacres [b.1937] was running a very successful estate agents business in Goring in 1939. Over the previous five years or so a large number of detached and semi-detached houses had been built on the old Goring Hall estate and business was brisk. However, the declaration of war changed everything. No more houses were built and no one wanted to buy a house on the 'invasion' coast. Janet's father was forced to move his family out of their smart new house in Sea Lane, Goring, and into a flat above the shops at Courtlands Parade.

Judy Hayden [b.1928] remembers her father's gloomy assessment of the likely impact of the war on the family's way of life:

I could see he was terribly gloomy and depressed – and me, aged 10, said to him, 'What's the matter Daddy?' And he just answered and said, 'I can tell you that life will never be the same again.'

Another family for whom life would never be the same again were the Simpsons, who lived in the large, classical-style house, 'Heslington', on Richmond Road. The family had several live-in servants, who lived in a separate wing of the house, as well as a cook and a gardener. However, the war changed their situation entirely. There was a demand that rooms should be made available to evacuees and many of the servants were called away to war work.

The family decided to rent out 'Heslington' and move into a smaller, rented house in Christchurch Road. They now only had one servant who cooked meals for the family, until she too was called up to do war work. This, Jacqueline Simpson [b. 1930], recalls posed a major challenge for her mother, who had never had to undertake domestic duties such as cooking, before. She recalls that the cook had been given one month's notice:

. . . and during that month she took my mother into the kitchen and started training her. So mama learned to cook partly from [the maid] and partly from the cookery classes that were springing up everywhere. The Gas Board ran cookery classes. The Electricity Board ran cooking classes. All the Women's Institutes and adult education and things – everyone went into cookery classes because everywhere there were women who had to cook for the first time in their lives . . . I remember an early disaster – her first attempt at potatoes; and it was a disaster because she did not realise the potatoes had to be of roughly equal sizes. She had some big ones and some little ones, and the little ones fell into mush and the big ones were still as hard as iron, and she couldn't make out why.

Fortunately, the cook was able to explain that the potatoes needed to be cut up into equal sized portions to cook evenly. Despite this unpromising start, Mrs Simpson rose to the challenge and by Christmas 1940 had produced, after very careful study, a perfectly fine Christmas cake.

One other middle class casualty of the leveling effect of war was none other than WCSS' own Honorary Secretary, Mrs Methold. The Executive Committee minutes books from the war years reveal what for Mrs Methold must have been a very embarrassing and awkward situation. Although the information in the archive is not specific, it would seem that the circumstances of war had badly impacted upon her husband's insurance business. Effie Methold had never drawn a salary for her full-time role with

V.E. Day celebrations outside Worthing Town Hall. Bomb-damaged walls can be seen in the immediate foreground.

WCSS but now, 'due to her personal circumstances', she was forced to write to the Executive Committee asking for a payment of £150 a year, until such time as she was able to work again without a salary.[9]

Her request was very modest, as some years later typists at WCSS were earning the amount she requested. After referring the matter to the Finance Committee, the Executive agreed to pay Mrs Methold the salary she had asked for, but described it as an 'honorarium', perhaps in recognition of the fact that the real professional salary for the work she did would have been far in excess of £150. The committee also agreed to pay her any 'out-of-pocket expenses'.[10] It is not recorded how long this payment continued but we can be sure it was for no longer than Mrs Methold believed to be absolutely necessary.

Whatever her personal situation, it in no way diminished Effie Methold's determination that WCSS should be at the cutting edge of providing the best social service provision in the country. Following the declaration of war, the National Council of Social Service, at the request of the government, called for the setting up of a Citizens' Advice Bureau, (CAB), in every town in the country. The very next day, the Worthing

'Dig for Victory' was the clarion call to the civilian population during the war. Manor Recreation Ground was cultivated at this time, and the remnants of the Brussels-sprout crop can plainly be seen in this photograph.

Citizens' Advice Bureau, run and organised by Mrs Methold, opened for business. In its first year of operation it dealt with 953 enquiries and in the second year that number increased to 2,908.[11]

The volunteer workers at the CAB had to be quick learners, as they grappled, on an almost weekly basis, with new government legislation, the vaguaries of war, and the need to liaise with numerous official bodies and authorities, including the military. At that time, the most common requests for information included: information regarding dependants' allowances, service questions, hire purchase, rent, housing, mortgages, national health insurance, old age pensions, evacuation, refugees, domestic problems, prisoners of war, missing relatives, children's cases, unemployment, distress caused by air raids damage and advice as to compensation.[12]

By 1942, WCSS was also offering free legal aid to members of the Armed Forces, with three Worthing solicitors giving their services free of charge. A Postal Message Scheme was established by which WCSS ensured that letters from Worthing people to relatives in enemy-occupied territories or in prisoner-of-war camps were delivered via the Red Cross. During the year 1940/41, 1,265 messages were sent from Worthing and 426 replies were received.[13] There was especial excitement in Worthing in May 1941 when nearly 200 letters from relatives in German-controlled Jersey arrived in the town. Mrs Lillian Parkerwood of 86 Westcourt Road, Worthing, was one of those who received a letter after almost a year of no news. She told the *Worthing Gazette*, 'I can't say how much we have been worrying, but it is all right now thanks to the Citizens' Advice Bureau and the International Red Cross, who are just wonderful.'[14]

The Allotments Scheme, started during the Depression, whereby WCSS helped to provide tools and seeds, etc., for the unemployed, was invigorated by the emergency of war, as the country sought to maximise its production of food and its drive to become self-sufficient, in what became known as the 'Dig for Victory' campaign. WCSS reported that many soldiers' wives had joined the scheme, taking over the plots their husbands

West Tarring School was being built when war broke out in 1939. Before any pupils were received, boys from Sussex Road School grew vegetables on what would later be sports fields, as Ernie Blackman, quoted below, recalls.

had tended before being called away to war.[15] Allotments remained crucial to the war effort not only throughout the period of hostilities but also into the lean 'austerity' years that followed. Jennifer Green [b.1939] remembers helping her stepmother on their allotment:

> *I think it was by Elm Grove in West Worthing by the railway line. How she managed to do this I don't know as she was not always a very well woman. I used to go there of an evening with her, taking a fork and a spade on our bikes. Not riding the bikes – they took the weight of it – and we used the baskets on the front to bring vegetables home that she had grown. My father went once to do a bit of digging but mainly it was my [step] mother. She was a very hard worker.*

The allotments at West Worthing still exist today, as do many of the wartime sites, whilst others were only ever designed to be temporary for the duration of the war. For instance, Manor Recreation Ground was turned over to cultivation as were the playing fields at the new school for boys at Tarring, as Ernie Blackman [b.1929] remembers:

> *... during the war the West Tarring school was being built and pupils would go from Sussex Road [school] to West Tarring for a gardening lesson which meant 'digging for victory', which meant you dug and planted the grounds of West Tarring school – which later became sports grounds – were all dug up and all made into vegetable plots to produce food for the people, that they could buy from the potting shed. So we grew vegetables in West Tarring, long before the school opened.*

Those old enough to remember tend to have very clear recollections of the day that war was declared. Most people remember the radio broadcast by the Prime Minister, Neville Chamberlain, announcing Britain was at war with Germany. Others recall the air raid sirens being sounded shortly afterwards, although it was to be a year before any actual raids took place. Ernie Blackman and a friend had taken their go-cart down

Anti-tank blocks on the seafront just to the east of Splash Point. By the time this photograph was taken in early 1945 the barbed wire and other defences had already been removed.

to the beach that early September morning, and it is from the perspective of a partly comprehending ten-year-old boy that Ernie recalls that first day of war:

> *I was down the beach with a friend of mine – Harry Lewis – and we were swimming and we heard the siren going and there was an old gent swimming down there with us, and we heard the siren going, and I said to Harry, 'That means gas. If you keep diving under the water it won't touch us.' So we kept diving under the water and this old boy says to us, 'You lads go home'. So we rushed out of the sea and we got dressed and the truck was waiting at the top. I got in the truck and Harry pushed me down Windsor Road and as we went down Chester Avenue, where I lived, past the school, everybody's outside their gate, looking up into the sky. . . .*

Although Worthing did not see any enemy action for a year, it did, within days, have to deal with a massive humanitarian crisis – the arrival in the town of over 10,000 evacuees from London.[16] This great movement of people from the capital to towns all along the south coast was driven by the fear that gas and bombing attacks on London might be imminent. Worthing had already had some experience of dealing with refugees, but nothing on this scale.

As explained in the previous chapter, Worthing had welcomed many Basque refugees, fleeing the fascists in Spain in 1937; and in the months before the outbreak of war, more child refugees came into Worthing, this time Jews fleeing Nazi persecution in Germany, Austria and those parts of Czechoslovakia occupied by the Germans. Hans Albrecht [b.1931] was part of the famous *kindertransport*, the concerted effort by Jews and others to get Jewish children out of the Nazi-controlled areas before the outbreak of war. Many non-Jewish families took in these children, including families in Worthing. The local refugee committee was run by Joan Strange who, along with her sister Kathleen, was well known in the town over many decades for their work on behalf of refugees, displaced persons and the homeless.

Hans was brought up in Austria but by the time he left in May 1939, the country of his birth was no longer a safe place for Jews to live. Hans first went to stay with a lady in Hove but she did not wish to keep him because he was handicapped and so, on 1 August 1939, Hans came to live in a refugee hostel at 73 Canterbury Road, Worthing, where he received a far warmer welcome. He remembers the people who ran the refugee committee in Worthing with fondness, including Joan Strange and Dr Morgenstern. However, he was an eight-year-old boy alone in a foreign country, not knowing what had become of his family in Austria.

Remarkably, Hans' mother managed to get out of Austria after the war commenced. Hans remembers that his mother left, 'with nothing but the things she had on her body,' on board an English river-boat, the *Lord Byron*, which took her to Romania. Eventually, in April 1940, she arrived in England and was reunited with her son. Mother and son went to live in lodgings in Lincoln Road but later that year they were forced to move out of Worthing. With a seaborne invasion a distinct possibility, anyone considered an 'enemy alien' was either interned or moved away from the coastal districts. As Austrians, albeit Jews, Hans and his mother fell into this category, and although not interned, they were obliged to move frequently over the next few years and 'went all over England'. However, they eventually returned to Worthing in 1946 and lived happily in the town for many years.

WCSS was heavily involved in looking after the welfare of refugees in Worthing, although some disagreement appears to have arisen with the Dental Section Committee of WCSS in September 1939 regarding the amount of assistance that the committee was giving to refugees. The minutes show that some members 'thought too much was being done for them' and that more refugees were being treated than local people. The committee resolved to ask the refugee committee to make a contribution to the cost of the refugees' dental treatment.[17]

Overall though, WCSS remained steadfast in its support for refugees. Mrs Methold, in her role as organiser of the CAB, took up many issues on behalf of the refugees, including writing letters for those who were not able to write fluently, or at all, in English. It was said that, 'In Worthing the refugees have a capable and helpful correspondent in the person of Mrs Bernard Methold.' It was also reported that WCSS was concerned about the 'renewed persecution of the Jews in Central Europe and other occupied countries', although no one could have imagined how terrible that persecution would become. By January 1944, there were 51 Jewish children living in Worthing, 27 of whom were at school, 14 at work and two were attending evening classes.[18]

Within a week of the outbreak of war, Worthing was accommodating thousands of evacuee children, sometimes accompanied by mothers and teachers. They came down by train and were greeted at the railway station by the local police, who passed them on to volunteers who were waiting to escort them to their new homes. Worthing policeman Bob Copper [b.1915] remembered those two or three days as being some of 'the hardest physical work' of his career:

> *They arrived on the top platform at Worthing Central and there were about six of us in*
> *uniform. And you just grab a couple of kids – poor little devils, you know, all bewildered*
> *– you just grab a couple and run under and up the steps and dump them up and*
> *somebody would take them off – and two more, and two more. And I remember the*
> *fleas, we were covered in fleas.*

Recent school leavers were called back to help escort the children to their new homes. Many people interviewed for this project recalled how lost and bewildered many of the children looked. Memories of the evacuees differ, but all agree that they were very poor children, from the East End of London, for whom even working class homes in Worthing seemed a luxury. There are many stories, usually second-hand, that relate the ignorance and lack of social skills amongst the evacuees, some which may be the result of prejudice or be the result of exaggeration in the retelling. Graham Bishop [b.1932] remembered being told that an elderly couple in Arlington Avenue in Goring, who had two evacuee children billeted with them, were astonished to learn that the children had never slept in beds before. Dorothy Till [b.1921] was told by her neighbours that their evacuee children were not sure whether to sleep on top of the bed or under the bed, and they thought it a terrible waste of space to leave the area under the bed unoccupied.

Peter Lock [b.1924] remembers that his family took in a Mrs Tapp and her three children, and then later took another two children from a different family. Despite so many people being squeezed into their terraced house in Ashdown Road, Peter remembers no problems and that 'it was really like a big family'. Arthur Linfield, one

The Old Town Hall during the war years. 'Pillbox' defences of reinforced concrete can be seen to the right of the picture and also on the roundabout in front of the town hall.

of the founders of WCSS, took in three children to his home in Thakeham. All across the town, people of all classes and backgrounds took in evacuees. Susan George recalled the hunger and shyness of the new arrivals:

Our first meal together had to be fish and chips because my mother was not prepared. Those children put their arms around the plates as if they were going to snatch them away. They were starving. My mother had quite a time showing them how to eat properly. It was ages before they would talk.[19]

Kathleen Skeet [b. 1929], who lived with her family in London, happened to be staying with relatives in Worthing when war broke out:

We stayed with my aunt in Brougham Road, and we stayed for a fortnight, and during that fortnight the war broke out. So my mother said, 'Well, we're going to move down here now, we'll be evacuees down here.' So mother and my father were in one place and my sister Pat and I, we were lodging with Mr & Mrs Duke, who lived in Brook Lane [Ferring]. And they were so good to us. They'd got a daughter my age and a son who was younger, and I always remember, they used to put their radio on the bottom of the stairs when we were in bed, and we could listen to ITMA, the Tommy Hanley programme, 'It's That Man Again', ITMA. There were three in the bed, mind you, my younger sister, myself and the girl Duke. In those days you never thought of it you know. A crowded family and it was a normal thing.

Within a few weeks of their arrival, the children were being integrated into Worthing life. They attended local schools, although at a different time to the local children, with one group going to school in the morning and the other in the afternoon. WCSS looked after the mothers' interests too. With the assistance of the Worthing Rotary Club and Rotary clubs in London, WCSS arranged for the prams of evacuated mothers to be brought down from London to Worthing. It had been observed that women were struggling around town, sometimes with two little ones in each arm, there having been no space on the trains for prams or pushchairs. Mrs Methold did, however, express her frustration at efforts being made to remove prams to Worthing for London mothers who, not liking Worthing, had returned to London without first informing WCSS.[20]

A canteen and social club were arranged for the mothers to attend, this being organised by WCSS Executive Committee member Mrs Rose Wilmot, assisted by the Worthing Towns-women's Guild (TWG).[21] The mayor visited the club in December 1939, when both mothers and children were present. Easing his way through the throng, he called out to them, asking, 'Are you down-hearted?', to which came back the hearty reply, 'No!'[22] The ladies of the TWG also helped by making clothes for the evacuee children. Many were too old or too delicate to undertake other wartime duties, such as firewatching, and felt they were 'doing their bit' by turning 'old coats, frocks and woollies' into trousers and dresses for the children. A Mrs Lee of Woodlea Road told a local reporter that she disliked firewatching, 'But I am able to get on with my sewing – it helps to keep me awake, so you see good does come out of evil.'[23]

Generally, relations between the Londoners and the Worthingites proved harmonious. Alfred Overington [b.1913] remembered that the evacuees 'soon fitted in'

These poor quality photographs show children in Worthing during the war. The top picture is of evacuees in Goring Woods and the bottom picture is of local lads dressed in makeshift uniforms and holding wooden rifles.

and that they 'mixed in very well'. There were, of course, exceptions. A number of cases of teenage evacuees indulging in petty crime and vandalism were reported to the police and several defendants appeared before Worthing magistrates to answer for these crimes. In December 1939, a hostel for delinquent children was opened at Woodlands in Poulters Lane to contain these unruly youngsters.[24]

If the mainly working class families who took in the bulk of the evacuee children were happy to do their bit to help out, there was sometimes a degree of exasperation with the attitude of some of the evacuees' relatives, who came down to visit them. Agnes Carter [b.1916] remembered that her husband would not sit down to eat dinner with the evacuee parents, because he did not think them 'very clean'. These same parents, Agnes recalled, would then spend the afternoon down the pub, rather than with their children. Susan George's mother, whose health was suffering under the strain of looking after her family, the evacuees and an aged parent, was none too impressed by the relatives of an evacuee called Ivy:

> *One day, her mother and uncle came down to see the children and what a poor little lady she was. The uncle was a horrible man. He smoked heavily and had the bad manners to stub out his cigarette on my mother's floor with his foot. She was horrified and was glad to see them go.*

When 'the blitz' started in August 1940 and invasion appeared inevitable, the evacuees from London were moved again, this time from Worthing to Yorkshire, where most of them stayed for the remainder of the war. Others, in spite of the bombing, decided to stay in London. Ivy's departure from the George household was tinged with the ambivalence that some Worthing people felt towards the London evacuees:

> *It was terrible to have to say goodbye. We were all crying. Ivy did not want to go. She had a big case full of clothes and presents and was carrying a lovely doll my mother had bought for her birthday and had dressed it beautifully. What a difference from when they arrived here. We had one letter to say they had arrived home safely and a long time later one more from Ivy. It was very badly written. Mum would not let me answer it as she thought they would be back to how they were before. Mum had dreaded the thought of what they would be going back to.[25]*

Having dealt very efficiently with the influx of evacuees, WCSS next turned its attention to what it believed to be were the town's inadequate preparations for war. In particular, it was concerned that there were not sufficient air raid shelters, that schools were unprepared and that there was no overall plan. Revd Haviland took up

Marine Drive at Goring, to the west of Sea Place. A road block is still seen to be in place, although this photograph was taken towards the end of the war. In 1940, at the height of the invasion scare, this was a restricted area, only freely accessible to the military.

the case and asked, 'What I want to know is why the Town Council does not take expert advice, and secondly what the Town Council expects the teachers and managers to do for the protection of the children if there are no trenches?'[26]

In the *Herald*, Frank Cave too took up the fight, lambasting the Council in an uncompromising fashion, 'Until the Council takes the first elementary steps of acquainting itself with the facts, it will remain open to the grave charge of trifling with a question affecting human lives.'[27] Shortly after these criticisms were made, Worthing appointed a new Town Clerk, who made the implementation of a defence plan a key priority. His son, Alan Townsend [b.1925], remembers his father placing all the town's sensitive documents in a chalk pit off Mill Lane in High Salvington. These were later removed to the Ralli mausoleum at South Farm Road cemetery.

After the fall of France in June 1940, Britain braced itself for invasion by Nazi Germany. Intelligence suggested that a seaborne invasion would take place on the south coast in September. Graham Bishop [b.1932] remembers how the threat of invasion impacted on middle class Goring:

> *My father [due to work commitments] had to stay and it was really quite, quite terrifying really, because we knew any moment we could be invaded. And back in the August of 1940, I well remember . . . a British major came round, an army major, and said that invasion was imminent and people were advised to leave. And that weekend practically everybody left Goring Hall estate. People had their cats and dogs put to sleep and they just went off to stay with friends or made other arrangements and the place was absolutely empty. We had to stay because my father had to stay, but it was eerie; we walked around the estate, there were no lights on, everybody had gone and we kept a full tank of petrol in the car, as you can imagine, and you expected invasion any day.*

As the professional people moved out, so the army moved in. Many large houses were taken over by the military, and the entire seafront was cordoned off with barbed wire and anti-tank blocks. A great earth ditch was dug around Worthing, designed to hinder any invasion force that might capture the town. Barriers made of scaffolding were erected, and no one without a pass could enter the town, which became very much under the sway of the military. Some local people found that their lives were now under the control of the armed forces, and that even their homes could be sacrificed for the war effort. Stella Sayers [b.1929] recalled the sometimes tense relationship between the military and the civilian population in Wallace Avenue:

> *I think mother had one bust up once. They said, 'If you lot start complaining we shall just clear you out and take over the property.' But nothing came of it, or I shouldn't be here now. But of course the top of the road, on this side of the road, the bend of Wallace Avenue which started Wallace Parade now, were all very big properties. – I think two were doctors' houses. As I say, all that side were big properties in their own grounds, but at the top there were very big properties, and they just took over the properties. And after a time of course they got different troops in. In the end they were given back to the people. There were no staircases, there were no banisters, there was nothing. They had ripped everything out to burn.*

In the spring of 1941, still believing that a German invasion of southern England was likely, it was decided to evacuate Worthing children to Mansfield in Nottinghamshire. This evacuation was not compulsory, although families were encouraged to send their children away from danger. By this time the town had experienced attacks by enemy planes and people in the town had been killed.

WCSS helped organise the evacuation and raised money to buy new clothes for

Military vehicles, possibly in Wallace Avenue, during the war. As Stella Sayers remembers (see above) the relationship between the army and the local residents was not always an easy one.

some of the poorer children who were to be evacuated. Mrs Methold believed that Worthing Town Council had promised to contribute to these costs, but this was later refuted by the mayor, who stated the council would not be able to contribute.[28] Once again WCSS was left on its own to bear the expense of its social work in the town.

Adge Roberts [b.1935], who was only five when he was evacuated with his older sister, recalls:

> We can both remember being dressed up in balaclava helmets and pixy hoods and scarfs and labels and thinking, 'Isn't this exciting, on this big outing we were going on; when, time we'd been gone 48 hours, we were crying our eyes out to come home again'.

Eileen Wright [b.1931] remembers that 'nobody wanted us' and that she was moved between three billets before she found people who 'were quite nice', but that 'the others were awful'. Ruby Peel [b.1927], although coming from a working class community in Orme Road, Worthing, thought it was 'awful' to see washing being hung up in the front gardens of houses in Mansfield. Pat Blackman [b.1936] was only five when she was evacuated with her four sisters, the youngest of whom was only three. Only her younger brother was kept at home in Worthing. Nonetheless, for Pat, being evacuated was 'fun in a way', and not altogether a bad experience.

Roger Davis [b.1929] was interested to observe the cultural differences between Worthing and Mansfield, not just in the work that people did but in the way they conducted themselves:

> [I was] living next door to a colliery and watching the cages going up and down all day, because it was only 50 yards from where we lived. I was staying with the fireman in charge of the brickworks, because every colliery in those days made bricks because what came up and wasn't used as coal was turned into bricks. So they had quite a big brick field next to the colliery. . . .
>
> . . . The people were quite different. We saw things you would never see in Worthing. Neighbours arguing over the wall – that sort of thing – and a crowd of about 30 watching. I had another friend, who was more in the centre of town – the colliery was sort of outside – and all sorts of things used to happen in the centre of town. Nothing too bad, but different from Worthing. If you had an argument up there, you had it out with your neighbour, whereas down here you kept quiet about it.

Susan George and her cousin were billeted with Mrs Keys, a 'crotchety lady' who they felt didn't like them and gave them meagre meals. She recalls that even the walk to school was nothing like anything she had experienced in Worthing:

The first day we went to school was a dreadful day with a thick blanket of smog, which is a mixture of smoke and fog and so dense that you cannot see your way. Mrs Keys said go straight down the road and you will come to High Oakham Girls' School. It must have been two miles; well it seemed very long and frightening as we edged along, my cousin and I holding tightly to one another. Then we heard some voices and called out to them to help us.[29]

While some Worthing children spent the rest of the war in Mansfield, others, homesick and unhappy, persuaded their parents to fetch them home again – not always an easy undertaking in wartime. One of those who returned home was Susan George and her cousin, and while it was good to be back home, the first day back at school in Worthing was a less than pleasant experience:

It was lovely to be back home with mum and dad and in my own bed. Mum kept saying how ill I looked. I had been picking holes in my face. It must have been nerves. The first day back at Davison's was embarrassing. We were all assembled in the hall and our headmistress, Miss Tate, a short plump lady, informed the school that we had let them down by coming home. We felt so small.[30]

For some youngsters evacuation was a great experience, for others less so. Most harrowing was the informant who spoke of the sexual abuse that she suffered from a member of the family she had been sent to live with. Sometimes danger is to be found in a mundane setting, rather than in the more obvious danger of a war zone.

This German fighter was shot down, north of Worthing, during the Battle of Britain in 1940.

Some of those children who did stay in Worthing during the war experienced the horror of bombing and death at first hand. Denis Spells [b.1931] saw a young woman killed when a German plane machine-gunned the town. He remembers seeing the pilot in the cock-pit and recalls, 'I was just scared stiff. I went home and they found me under the table in the kitchen.' Derek Porter [b.1929] recalls several incidents of enemy action in the town but one, in particular, sticks in his memory:

. . . the one I remember most vividly was one afternoon in 1940. I looked up – I was in Kingsland Road – and I looked up and I saw this aircraft approaching quite slowly from the east, travelling to the west – didn't deviate – a straight line, and then suddenly I saw the bomb doors open and several bombs drop out of it, and I thought, 'Blimey, what do I do?' So I dived under a flint wall by Hampton's Dairy which is on the corner of Wigmore Road and Kingsland Road – I think it's a private residence now, but it was Hampton's Dairy. . . . And there was an almighty explosion; as I stood up this woman came running up and put her arms round me and she said, 'My house has gone, my house has gone!' . . . and with that the smoke was clearing and the roof [of her house was visible] and with that she calmed down, she could see her house was still there, but what it had done, directly opposite the Wigmore Hotel, in Leigh Road, on the north side there was a bungalow and then there was a semi-detached house and a bomb fell there and it flattened the properties.

Bob Copper [b.1915] was in the temporary police station at the Art College in Union Place, when the first bomb to fall on Worthing hit Caffyns Garage in Chapel Road, opposite the town hall, in September 1940:

I was on duty down there, and it blew all the windows out from the blast that came off, and we were fast asleep on tables and in chairs and things, on duty, just having a doze, you know. And I put my blooming boots on and I couldn't for shaking – it's involuntary, it's just the shock. And I thought, 'This is silly, you've got to go out and be an example,' and I couldn't try to tie my bootlace up.

Later on during the war, Bob was twice blown off his feet by bomb blasts while on duty. Worthing was not the tranquil backwater in the Second World War that some might imagine.

Worthing CAB went to great lengths to keep loved-ones in touch with each other, including arranging for wives and mothers to visit wounded husbands and sons recovering in hospitals in other parts of the country. Sometimes wives were even able to visit non-wounded husbands quartered elsewhere in the country, if there were compelling personal reasons for

Worthing policeman, Bob Copper, on his bike in 1940. Bob, who later became a well-known folk singer and writer, recalled some close shaves with German bombs during the war.

doing so. The cost of travel and overnight stays were all borne by WCSS. Throughout this period, the generosity of subscribers allowed such good work to continue, indeed without it WCSS could not have continued, as grants from Worthing Town Council and West Sussex County Council were minimal, and, as we have seen, were sometimes withdrawn.

War is still portrayed in a heroic guise, and while most people are aware of the suffering and pain it causes, rarely is the anguish of ordinary soldiers revealed in books or newspaper articles. It seems right, therefore, that such memories should be recorded in this book. Two examples perhaps suffice to demonstrate that soldiers do not become 'heroes' simply by putting on a uniform. Mary Martin [b.1934] remembers the Canadian troops who were quartered in a commandeered hotel just around the corner from the family home in New Street:

> *Well, my mother told me that one night when the raids were on when the bombers came – you could hear them coming over – and there was one on duty, and they used to be on duty, walking up and down the road. And you could hear them. And she opened the door and he was crying. He'd come from a farm and he'd never heard anything, never heard gunfire, he was just 18. And he ended up in the Anderson [shelter] – we had an Anderson – and he ended up in there with us – he was so petrified. Mum said, 'You know, he's some mother's son.'*

Second World War gun emplacement at Worthing.

Many of these young Canadians were killed in the near suicidal 'Dieppe Raid' in 1942. Kathleen Skeet [b.1929] also recalled the fears of the young servicemen:

> *I got to know one soldier, although I was still in school still – and he was crying at the thought of having to go back and go through all the war again. My sister's husband, he suffered with shell-shock, and he came back for a rest period, but had to go back. And because we were having gunfire all the time – it was practice . . . every time he heard the gunfire practice he wouldn't believe it was practice. He was absolutely shaking with fear, he was terrified.*

Those who did survive the war were often deeply affected. Molly Cormick [b.1917]

told how her husband would never talk to her about his experiences. Michael Luck [b.1934] recalls that his father would never speak about what happened to him and that 'very few people spoke about the war.' John Sams [b.1922], who returned from the war in Burma, remembered that his health was broken and that he 'gave into every kind of infection'. Even after victory in 1945, there was a lot that needed to be done to rebuild shattered lives and to work towards a better society than the one people had known before the war.

As already stated, by 1942 the social deprivation that WCSS had been set up to tackle had dramatically diminished. In 1944, new, larger, offices were acquired at 22 Chapel Road. From this time forward WCSS devoted much of its time and resources

V.E. Day street party in Orme Road, May 1945. Notice the absence of men – most were still serving in the Forces at this time. Notice also how much more healthy and better dressed the people appear than in the Coronation street party (page 33), only eight years earlier.

to promoting other areas of social improvement. Between 1942 and 1945, WCSS launched initiatives to provide residential homes for the elderly; to promote the benefits of nursery education and to publish a report, *Homes of Tomorrow*, which sought to ensure that decent, reasonable priced housing would become a right rather than a privilege. Furthermore, a new 'section' was opened in Lancing, themes which will be explored in the following chapters.

In the concluding paragraph of its 1945 annual report, WCSS set out its vision for the future, and in particular the importance it attached to community centres, something very dear to the heart of WCSS members, Rose Wilmot and Sidney Walter:

> *Some of the main problems of the next few years will be centred round housing and the family. After the long years of war it is imperative that family life be revived and preserved. The need for full employment to ensure a livelihood and security has been recognised, but equally important is the need of some focal point, where the spirit of comradeship formed in the war years may be fostered – where recreational, educational, health and local government facilities are centred – in fact a building catering for all members of the family, from the youngest to the oldest.[31]*

Increasingly though, despite its broad remit, the following years and decades would see WCSS devote an increasing proportion of its activities to care services for the elderly, as the town's population continued to age at what some believed to be an alarming rate.

Free ice cream for all children
under 14 – a V.E. Day treat.

References

1 *Worthing Herald*, 11 May 1945

2 WCSS, Annual Report, 1939/40

3 WCSS, Annual Report, 1940/41

4 WCSS, Annual Report, 1941/42

5 *Worthing Herald*, 18 December 1942

6 WCSS, Annual Report, 1941/42

7 WCSS, Annual Report, 1940/41

8 WCSS, Annual Report, 1939/40

9 WCSS, Executive Committee minutes, 18 January 1943

10 Ibid. 8 February 1943

11 WCSS, Annual Report, 1940/41

12 WCSS, Annual Report, 1939/40

13 WCSS, Annual Report, 1940/41

14 *Worthing Gazette*, 28 May 1941

15 WCSS, Annual Report, 1939/40

16 Exact figure of 10,252 quoted in the *Sussex Daily News*, 5 December 1939

17 WCSS, Dental Section Committee minute book, 15 September 1939

18 *Worthing Herald*, 21 January 1944

19 George, Jean, *Parts of my Life* (self-published), p.10

20 *Worthing Herald*, 29 September 1939

21 *Worthing Gazette*, 18 October 1939, *Worthing Herald*, 20 October 1939

22 *Worthing Gazette*, 6 December 1939

23 *Worthing Herald*, 5 September 1941

24 *Sussex Daily News*, 5 December 1939

25 George, Jean, ibid, p.11

26 *Worthing Herald*, 12 January 1940

27 Ibid.

28 WCSS, Personal Services Committee minute book, 24 March 1941

29 George, Jean, ibid, p.16

30 Ibid.

31 WCSS, Annual Report, 1944/45

Three members of the Methold House Old People's Club, in 1962, return their empty cups to the volunteer tea lady. Modern-day Methold House is a little more sophisticated.

In 1970, when Arthur Linfield was over 80 years of age, he said that he regarded himself as 'old' but not as 'elderly', and he thought that ageing was all a state of mind and that he was still very active. So deciding when a person becomes 'old' is highly subjective. In writing this chapter, the author has tended to assume that 'old' includes people over the age of retirement, but then, for some people today, that could be 55 or younger – hardly an age many people would now regard as old. However, a look through some of the case files of the WCSS Personal Services Committee from the 1930s shows people being described as old or elderly at what we today would consider a surprisingly young age.

In 1933, the Personal Services Committee addressed itself to the problems of 'an elderly Scottish lady' who had fallen on difficult times. She had worked for many years as a matron in a children's ward of a large hospital. Increasing deafness had forced her to abandon that career and take up a new but less prestigious one as a cook, until this toil brought about a further and apparently irreparable collapse in her general health. The records state that she was 'an independent old lady' who was reluctant to accept help from WCSS. Eventually the committee was able to persuade her to accept their assistance and provide her with an allowance until she was eligible to claim the Old Age Pension. This would mean that the lady was in her early sixties or even late fifties.[1] (The women's retirement age of 60 was introduced in 1940.)

In 1936, 'an elderly man' who was in Worthing Hospital recovering from a serious operation was referred to the committee, as his doctor had recommended a long period of convalescence and after-care nursing, something the man was unable to provide for out of his meagre resources. The committee was able to pay these costs, including a six-week recuperation at WCSS' 'rest cottage' at Thakeham. (See chapter on Families and Communities.) After this protracted period of care and rest, the man 'was taken back by his former employer'.[2] We must assume then that he was of working age and therefore no older than 64.

Two years later, we read of 'two elderly sisters', one of whom was receiving a widow's pension, while the other worked to supplement this modest income. However, the second sister became ill and unable to work. Once again the committee stepped in to provide financial support until a time, 'a few years hence, when she was eligible for her old age pension'.[3] This woman, it would seem, was in her early sixties, yet was thought of as being elderly. These are only a few of the examples to be found in the minute books of the Personal Services Committee. When referring to a bed-ridden 'old lady' of 80, the writer of that year's annual report does so in a way that suggests that the very fact she had reached such an age was remarkable in itself and that her disability was only to be expected.[4]

Those older people interviewed as part of the 'Time for History' project, of which this book is a part, also recall 'old age' afflicting their grandparents at a far earlier time than would be expected today. Indeed, many of those interviewed had no recollection of their grandparents at all, as they had all died when the interviewee was very young or before they were born. Others recall immobile and remote figures, dressed in black, sitting in a chair, unable or unwilling to interact with their grandchildren. Joan Bishop [b.1929] remembered that her grandparents were either 'dead or dying'. Dorothy Till [b.1921] finds it hard to believe that her grandparents were in their 'sixties when they died, as she remembers them as being 'really old people'. Mina Dickinson, who was interviewed in 1991 when she was 74, recalled that her grandmother 'considered herself old when she was in her 50s.'[5] David O'Brien [b.1939], whose Welsh grandparents were both alive when he was a child, did not find them lively or endearing:

Members of Methold House Old People's Club, shortly after it opened in 1958. Men were as welcome to join as women, but in 1958 not many men lived to be 'old'.

They used to terrify me, 'cause she used to sit there dressed in black, and he sat there with his cap and his pipe and they could hardly speak any English.

Other interviewees noted how much earlier old age appeared to overcome people in their childhood, compared with their own experience as older people today. Margaret Hallard [b.1945] observed that:

Everyone looked much older than people do these days. I look at myself sometimes and think, 'Gosh, I'm 63 and what mum looked like when she was 43', but then look what she'd been through. She'd had a poverty stricken childhood and been through two world wars, so you can't expect them to look the same, can you?

The evidence of poverty and struggle given in the previous chapters of this book certainly reinforces Margaret's opinion. We have also seen, though, how many people's lives were improved during the Second World War and that this was particularly true for the elderly, with the introduction of the Supplementary Old Age Pension in 1940. Since the end of the war, older people have been able to enjoy a standard of living and healthcare provision undreamt of by previous generations, as well as being able to look forward to living many years past the age of retirement, without the spectre of the workhouse haunting their final days. Yet despite these gains, the workload of WCSS and later the Guild in regards to services for older people has increased considerably with each passing decade.

Cynthia Davey (née Street) with her sister Rosemary, dressed as bridesmaids, with a rather fearsome looking grandmother standing over them.

During the nineteenth century and the early part of the twentieth century, Worthing had a reasonably broad range of ages represented amongst its population. That there was a higher proportion of over 60s in the borough, compared to the national average, was testimony to the better living conditions here than those prevailing in the urban centres of London, the Midlands or the North. However, a considerable change was perceptible after the First World War, with Worthing becoming the town of choice for those seeking peaceful and congenial retirement.

An elderly gentleman, William Madgwick, in his garden around about 1930.

The town was flat and enjoyed a long coastline and promenade – amenities that were very attractive to potential residents seeking a new life outside of London.

During the war, many more elderly people came to Worthing to escape the bombing in London, finding relatively cheap accommodation in the boarding houses and hotels of the town. Worthing was a restricted area during the war years and access to holiday visitors was severely curtailed. The increasing number of older people in the town soon became an issue for WCSS, who had to contend with the particular problems that this new cohort of residents presented. As we shall see, before the war had ended, WCSS had established its first residential home for elderly people on low incomes in the town; yet after the war the problems became far more severe. Firstly, the number of over-60s in the population continued to grow, and secondly, the owners of guest houses and hotels, who had been happy to accept low rents from long-term guests during the war, expected them to vacate for holiday-makers paying higher summer tariffs once the war had ended.

By 1945 a quarter of the population of Worthing were over the age of retirement and by 1954 this had risen to 28.5%; by 1962 to over 33%.[6] Both the censuses of 1961 and 1971 revealed that Worthing had the oldest population in the country. In 1961, Bexhill was a distant second, with 23% of its population being over retirement age. Bournemouth had a higher number of older people but, as a proportion of the total population, they represented 21%. In 2009, those aged over 65 represented 23% of the national population. Not until about 2040 will the country as a whole record the same proportion of people aged over 65 that Worthing was experiencing in the 1960s.[7] These are quite remarkable statistics and explain why it was that increasingly WCSS, and later the Guild, found more and more of its time being spent on issues concerning older residents.

WCSS tried to retain a broad and diverse range of services, but the demands of an ever-ageing population made this desire impossible to fulfil. In 1953 the annual report confidently asserted that, 'It must be stressed that the Council is concerned with and works for all the community, and not primarily for the old.'[8] Yet by 1956, there was already an acceptance that this might not be achievable, 'Because of the nature of Worthing and the high proportion of elderly and aged residents, our work for old people has taken, and must continue to take, an important place in our programme.'[9]

A group of elderly ladies chatting. This photograph is difficult to date, but is probably from the 1960s. Also difficult to determine is the location; could it be by the Old Town Hall?

WADCOSS introduced its first minibus in 1967, although they called it an ambulance and had a flashing light on top. Guild Care's modern vehicles are a lot less clinical.

As we shall see, WCSS sought to respond to the challenge of an ageing population by opening a series of high-quality residential homes for older people – homes that would later include provision for nursing as well as providing accommodation and catering. There were also campaigns to increase the number of geriatric hospital beds in the town, and to open clubs and day centres for the active elderly. These initiatives and campaigns hugely increased the provision and quality of facilities for older people in the town, but the gains were always being made against a rising tide of demand, or as Frank Cave put it in 1983, 'It seems at times that little progress has been made, for the aged population has gone on multiplying, and the provision has numerically become greater.'[10] Of course, without the intervention of WCSS/Guild Care, the position would have been immeasurably worse. Indeed there would have been something of a social catastrophe in the town.

This immense pressure placed on the caring services – both state and voluntary – caused some in the town to ask whether a halt should not be called to the number of older people coming to retire to Worthing. In 1958, the Revd Hubert Janisch, a much respected clergyman in the town, warned that Worthing was becoming 'a mecca for old people', and that this trend could not be sustained indefinitely.[11] In 1965, *New*

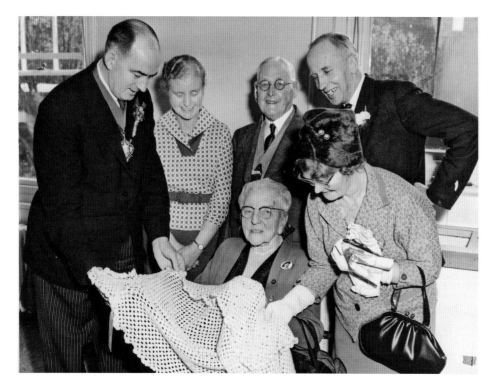

Mrs Louisa Brunwin receives guests on her 105th birthday in 1965. She was the first centenarian to live in one of WADCOSS' homes. She still liked to crochet, and is seen holding a shawl she had made. She hit the headlines when she went to vote at the 1964 election, with her 'young friend' Mr Hastings (also pictured), a mere 92! Reaching such an advanced age was considered quite remarkable at the time, but today Guild Care has several centenarians living in its homes.

Society magazine ran an article warning its readers that what was happening in Worthing today would be replicated across the country as a whole in the future. 'The danger facing a town like Worthing is that it may become one vast old people's ghetto, run by old people for old people, its minority of young people simply opting out of the whole business.'[12]

Even Joseph Sayers, Secretary of Worthing and District Council of Social Service (WADCOSS – as it was known from 1958), was reported as saying that he was against the continued flow of elderly people into the town.[13] Sayers had been addressing a meeting of Worthing Young Liberals and the report of the meeting had been sent to the local newspapers by their press secretary, Roger Sutton. In a letter to the press, Sayers denied having made the alleged remark, but instead went on to list all the work that was being done by WADCOSS to help older people in Worthing, including the fact that 87% of its funds were spent on provision for the elderly.[14]

There were older people in Worthing who felt increasingly under attack and some strong-worded letters from irate readers were published in the Worthing newspapers. One correspondent declared that, 'These headlines make us feel like Hitler's unwanted Jews.'[15] Another wrote, directly attacking Sayers, demanding to know if he would be taking his own advice 'when anno Domini catches up with him', and leave the town, rather than adding to the retired population.[16] Roger Sutton still recalls the controversy, 46 years later, and is adamant that Sayers never spoke the words attributed to him in the *Herald*, and that the controversial phrase had not been included in his original press release.

What makes this incident all the more curious is that Frank Cave was editor of the *Worthing Herald* at the time. Why would he have run an inaccurate story that was bound to cause Joseph Sayers embarrassment? Roger Sutton remembers Sayers telling him that Cave was always causing him problems in the press and that Cave 'seemed to delight in causing trouble for him'.[17] It is certainly true that Sayers was often the focus of controversy and, as we shall see in later chapters, he was reported as holding what might today be termed 'robust' views on young people, women and the future use of churches. Was he being constantly misreported or was he something of a loose cannon?

In his booklet on the Guild, published in 1983, Frank Cave gave a fulsome tribute to Joseph Sayers, who had died a few years earlier, commending his years of devoted service and describing him as being a worthy successor to Mrs Methold. He went on to praise his many talents and the long hours of work he put in every week. And

In 1958 Worthing Rotary Club, always a great supporter of WADCOSS, agreed to sponsor an annual holiday for elderly people with small incomes. For many years the Isle of Wight was the chosen destination. This photograph shows a holiday group about to board the Isle of Wight ferry; for many of them this would have been their first trip 'overseas'.

although he does say that Sayers was 'not, perhaps, a great administrator', he lauds him as 'a man of immense compassion'.[18] Whatever the truth, the reporting of Sayers' supposed comments in 1963 caused, as Roger Sutton remembers, quite a stir in the town.

In 1969 it was *The Times*, not the *Worthing Herald*, that reported Sayers as saying that people about to retire should not come to Worthing unless they were well provided for financially, advising that, 'It is better to stay where you are known.'[19] These comments reflected the desperate lack of suitable accommodation in the town at that time, as well as the practice of some landlords, who would evict older residents if they thought they could get higher rents from other tenants. In 1970, Thames Television ran a documentary entitled, 'All Our Miss Stedmans', in which it was alleged that many old people in Worthing were living in cramped, poorly equipped and over-priced accommodation and that the health and caring services were unable to respond adequately to the need. Although Councillor Reg Callender declared that the pro-gramme was 'simply denigrating Worthing in a shocking fashion',[20] there were others who felt that the programme-makers were exaggerating to make a valid point.

In 1971, the Local Authority Social Services Act came into force, with the result that, locally, many services for the elderly that had been supplied on an ad hoc basis or by several authorities and organisations were now, in theory at least, to be co-ordinated through the new West Sussex Social Services, operated by West Sussex County Council. Although some within WADCOSS resented this new creation, seeing it as an attempt to usurp their own work of 40 years standing, the change did allow WADCOSS to focus on its strengths, rather than attempt to offer more services than it had the capacity to deliver. We will return to post-1971 developments later in this chapter, after considering the work of WCSS, later WADCOSS, in providing residential homes and retirement clubs in the town, and its campaign for improved geriatric nursing care.

Before the Second World War, private nursing homes offered care to those who could afford it, and for those who were able-bodied there was the option of spending their final days in a boarding house or hotel, assuming they had no family to take care of them. For poorer people the choice was very stark – either live with relatives or go to the workhouse. For many poorer families the burden of looking after an aged or infirm relative put profound strain on family relationships and finances. Barbara Windeatt [b.1937] remembers that her blind grandmother would stay at her parents' home for three months and then be moved on to another branch of the family. In truth it was the short life expectancy of elderly relatives that made this type of arrangement feasible.

Methold House in 1962. The facilities and décor seem so drab and basic compared to those now at Methold House.

Today, Guild Care runs four residential homes in Worthing: Caer Gwent, Ashmount, Irene House and Linfield, which has a specialist unit for those with dementia. It also runs the Dolphin Court retirement flatlets. The very first home was opened at 4 Church Walk in 1943, and although many individuals within WCSS were responsible for what was then a bold and exciting departure for a voluntary sector charity, it was Frank Cave as the chairman of the Old People's Homes sub-committee who was the driving force behind making the dream a reality.

In December 1941, Miss E. Samson of the National Council of Social Service spoke to WCSS' AGM on the subject 'Old People's Homes and Welfare'.[21] This talk appears to have inspired the members of the WCSS Executive Committee to see what steps could be taken to open a home for the elderly on low incomes in Worthing. In April 1942, Mrs Methold reported to the committee that she had seen what could be a suitable property at 30 Christchurch Road; what was more, a local businessman, Mr Charles Whitcomb, Chairman of Messrs. Potter, Bailey and Co. Ltd., had offered to pay the asking price of £1,200. However, the excitement caused by these developments soon turned to disappointment when a structural survey revealed that the property had significant problems with its drains, and the sale was abandoned.

However, Mr Whitcomb had been so impressed with the energy and commitment shown by WCSS in pursuing its goal of providing low-cost residential care in

4 Church Walk, the first residential home for older people, opened by WCSS in 1943.

Worthing, that he offered a substantial property, already in his ownership, to WCSS – 4 Church Walk. Mr Whitcomb, who had risen from humble origins to be one of the town's foremost businessmen, stipulated that his gift was to be treated as an anonymous donation and that he wanted no public recognition. The committee was also told that another anonymous donor was prepared to equip the house with all the furnishings and equipment it would require. This donor turned out to be WCSS' recently retired President, Sir Arthur Newsholme, who died before the home could be opened.

The official opening of 4 Church Walk took place on 17 September 1943. The opening ceremony was performed by Mrs Bell, the wife of the Bishop of Chichester, with the local MP, Earl Winterton, in attendance. It had been hoped to provide accommodation for fifteen elderly ladies but, due to a lack of facilities, there were usually only twelve ladies in residence in the early years of the home's existence. Despite the generosity of its benefactors, 4 Church Walk did lack many facilities that today would be regarded as essential, including adequate heating in some of the bedrooms. All the residents had to share, with up to four ladies in a bedroom, depending on redecoration and other works taking place within the house. Forty years later, Frank Cave recalled how volunteers got on their hands and knees to scrub floors and lay carpets, although there was not enough carpet for all the rooms.[22] Nor were there sufficient curtains for every window. Screens had to be borrowed from Worthing Hospital to act as temporary curtains.[23]

During the war years, Mr Dillistone, the local ARP warden, was a regular visitor, reassuring the ladies of their safety following air raid alerts. Also popular was the Revd Neal Snelling, who was honorary chaplain to the home. Dr Taylor, Medical Advisor to WCSS, suggested that potential residents should be given one month's trial, as it was not possible for him to assess the suitability of applicants on the basis of one medical examination.[24] Only those in reasonable health could be admitted to the home and, once admitted, they could only remain so long as they did not require nursing care. The only medicine permitted on the premises appears to have been a bottle of brandy, which was in the possession of the matron, who was supposed to record all uses made of it by the residents.[25] Furthermore, visitors were reminded that it was not permitted to bring alcohol on to the premises.[26]

Taken as a whole, the WCSS/Guild Care story is one of success and of impressive, hard-working individuals who made that success possible. However, not everything has run smoothly over a period of over seventy-six years, and perhaps no period was more regrettable and unhappy than the years 1944–1950 at the Church Walk Home. A lesser organisation might have despaired and given up the idea of running a home altogether, rather than setting its sights on opening new and bigger homes.

Only the minute books of the Executive Committee and the Old People's Home Committee give the details of what occurred during those years. The annual reports talk vaguely of 'staffing difficulties', a phrase used by Edward Kellett in his history of the Guild. Frank Cave makes no mention at all of the series of calamities that befell the Church Walk Home. The story of what happened is rather extraordinary, and at times disturbing, although it does have a happy ending.

The dining room at 4 Church Walk – a homely scene that gives no clue to the alleged cruelty taking place at the home in 1949.

The first matron, Miss Richardson, resigned in February 1944 after only five months in post. She was then replaced by a Mrs Baxendale, although it is not clear if she ever took up the appointment, for by May 1944, Mrs Lawrence was reported to be in post on a three-month trial as matron, although by October she had been replaced by Amy Steven. There then followed a number of appointments of assistant matrons, one of whom sailed for Canada after just one day's employment. In June 1945, Mrs Bremner was appointed matron, but by October had been replaced by Miss B-----d. No reason for this rapid turnover of staff is given.

In 1946, WCSS opened their second and larger residential home, Caer Gwent in Wykeham Road. Miss B-----d successfully applied for the post of matron of the new home, leaving Church Walk once again without a matron. Several potential applicants for the matron's post turned down the job when it was offered to them. The committee decided to raise the salary from £120 to £150 a year, with a promise of £180 in the second year. Miss Leveridge was appointed, but shortly afterwards was found to be unsuitable and 'given immediate notice'.[27] A series of temporary matrons then followed, during which time WCSS was very much distracted with its problems at Caer Gwent.

A special sub-committee was established to look into the running of Caer Gwent and gave Miss B-----d a list of its concerns. It was said there had been adverse criticisms of her management of the home, including her attitude towards the residents and that she had refused to work with the Red Cross, who were supposed to be providing nursing care.[28] At a special meeting of the Executive Committee, Miss B-----d was asked to resign. Following her resignation, Mrs Methold reported the loss of linen and silverware from the Church Walk Home. The committee asked the honorary solicitor, Mr Cushing, to write to Miss B-----d asking if 'she could throw any light on the subject'.[29] When no satisfactory answer was received, the matter was reported to the police and an investigation launched. The outcome of this investigation is not reported in the minutes.

Although Caer Gwent had a new matron by July 1947, in the person of Mrs Eastwood, the Church Walk post was still vacant. It was reported that a matron had resigned in September 1947, due to ill health, but no name was given. The following month, Mrs Ann Bush turned down an offer of employment 'on doctor's orders'.[30] Due to lack of staff, the home had to be temporarily closed and the residents re-housed 'at considerable expense'.[31] In quick succession a number of matrons were offered the post and turned it down or were judged unsuitable. Mrs Cull was offered a month's trial in January 1948, after which the committee 'decided to dispense with her services forthwith'.[32]

Residents at Caer Gwent
residential home in the 1950s.

In June 1948, Mrs B------y was appointed on a three-month trial and then, perhaps somewhat unexpectedly, given all that had gone before, she was confirmed in post two months later. The problems did not end for Church Walk – other staff left, one storming out on Easter Monday. The matron asked the committee to sack the cook as she was 'slip-shod'.[33] A new cook was sent on a course to learn pastry and cake-making. The matron became dissatisfied with the woman and she was dismissed with one week's notice.

This high turnover of employees might appear farcical but the events of 1949 proved all too grave. In March 1949, Mrs Methold reported that she had received complaints from relatives as to how Mrs B------y had been treating the residents of the home. It was agreed that Mrs Peryer should investigate and report back to the committee.[34] It appears that the claims could not, at that time, be substantiated. However, in August, while Mrs B------y was on holiday, terrible stories began to emerge from the home about the way in which the matron had been treating residents. The committee was informed that there was 'an air of terror among the old people' and that they were frightened at the prospect of the matron's return.[35]

Although the committee decided to dismiss Mrs B------y, they did not inform her of their decision, but secretly sought to find a replacement. In the meantime, Mrs B------y demanded new curtains for her bedroom and yet another cook resigned. The committee's plans were discovered by Mrs B------y, when a potential applicant for her job arrived at Church Walk, announcing herself as the new matron and asking probing questions. A furious Mrs B------y then confronted Mrs Methold, demanding to know why she was to be dismissed. Mrs Methold refused to discuss the matter with her but reported the events to the committee, who finally took the decision to give Mrs B------y notice. The committee gave four reasons for dismissal, including her age, (not a reason an employer could use today), that she was lazy and was unable to deal with emergencies; but they did not specify the allegations of cruelty and bullying made by the residents.[36]

Perhaps with its appalling reputation, it is not surprising that WCSS received 'very few replies' to its advert for a new matron at Church Walk.[37] Only two candidates were interviewed, but one of them, Miss Nora Gammans, was judged to be 'most suitable'[38] and so it proved to be, for not only did Miss Gammans pass her trial period, but after a year's service, the committee commended 'her excellent work' and raised her salary to £180. She remained in post for 23 years, retiring at the age of 70 in 1973.

In his history, Edward Kellett, while skirting over the troubles of the early years at Church Walk, did not stint on the significance of Miss Gammans' appointment for WCSS, which he regarded as a 'turning point' and one that would have 'an everlasting effect'. Kellet may not have wished to record the bad times, but his comment that, 'So followed a period of much happiness and contentment,'[39] really does speak for itself.

Nora Gammans stands very much in the tradition of service that characterised the founders of WCSS. Her mother, a past chairman of Lancing Parish Council, had been a founding member of the short-lived 'Lancing Section' of WCSS. Miss Gammans remembered her 'strict Methodist upbringing', which included charitable giving. She remembered that it was not unusual for her father to bring home 'someone in need' to share a meal at the family table.[40] As a young woman she moved to London and was working for Kingston Borough Council during the war years. She returned to Lancing to help look after her ailing father, and it was then that she saw the post of matron at Church Walk advertised.

Miss Nora Gammans, matron of 4 Church Walk and then Whitcomb House from 1950 to 1973. She transformed the home, ensuring it became a place of happiness rather than fear.

In 1953, Miss Gammans oversaw the removal of the residents to a new home in Selden Road, just round the corner from Church Walk. This was named 'Whitcomb House', in memory of the home's benefactor. A major rebuilding and extension programme in 1967 created modern, single bedrooms, providing accommodation for 33 elderly men and women. Miss Gammans said that it was a love of humanity that motivated her, and the happy home she created at Whitcomb House was certainly testimony to that creed. On her retirement in 1973, Miss Gammans reflected on the changes that she had seen in the care for the elderly in her lifetime – years that began with old age being haunted by the spectre of the workhouse and culminated in the friendly surroundings of Whitcomb House:

Miss Gammans welcomes a new resident to Whitcomb House.

People as they got past looking after themselves had to be taken into official care. To come to a place like Whitcomb House filled them with a sense of gratitude, and as many of them were in their 60s it was like a big family. They enjoyed being in a home. Today it is all a bit different. People stay in their own homes much longer, supported by the social services, meals on wheels and home helps. When they come to us they are really too old to stay alone even with this help – and, very old to adapt to change. Also, attitudes have changed and so have people. They have 'rights' these days. But by and large we have been a happy crowd. . . .[41]

Alan Gunn [b.1927], has been a supporter of the Guild for many years, and served on the old committees. He too remembers that whereas at one time people would enter a home in their 70s or even late 60s, and that it was quite usual for them to be active, undertaking chores, such as 'a bit of dusting, polishing and tidying up' in the home, today they are much older and more infirm. The most recent data from Guild Care shows that the average age of residents in its homes is 88 years[42] – an age very few people could have imagined living to when the Council of Social Service was first established in 1933.

Caer Gwent, previously mentioned and opened in 1947, provided a home for both men and women and could also offer nursing care, provided by the Red Cross, (although as we have seen, the first matron of the home appeared less than enthusiastic about this relationship). Preference for residency was given to people who had suffered through bombing, had served in the war or had lost relatives in the war.

The original Caer Gwent in Wykeham Road, which was later removed to a property in Belsize Road, and then to the current location in Downview Road. Guild Care's newest home, Linfield, stands on the site of the first Caer Gwent.

Furthermore, potential residents had to be living in Worthing or other localities covered by WCSS' remit.[43] Applications would only be considered from people with a weekly income of less than £3 10s and capital not exceeding £1,500.[44]

Many improvements were made to Caer Gwent over the years. In 1954, a donation of £4,000 paid for the construction of an extension, know as the Clarice Griffin Wing.[45] In 1959 'wireless relay' was installed in the bedrooms, allowing the residents to listen to their favourite radio programmes.[46] It was very clear that even with the increased capacity of Whitcomb House and Caer Gwent, a third home was desperately needed. Several properties were considered, but every time WADCOSS was outbid by property developers. Finally, in 1962, successful negotiations were entered into to purchase the Ashmount Hotel in Shelley Road. The Rotary Club was able to donate £10,000 to the appeal to raise the necessary £45,000 to complete the purchase.[47]

The appeal was very successful and the town was urged to make 'the cash mount for Ashmount'. The home was officially opened by Dame Sybil Thorndike on 12 June, 1963. Dame Sybil, who had broadcast on the radio for donations to the appeal, said she was delighted that the appeal fund was only £2,100 short of its target, at which

The official opening of Ashmount residential home in 1963 by Dame Sybil Thorndike. Arthur Linfield is seen standing next to Dame Sybil, with the Mayor behind her. The clergyman wearing the glasses is the Revd Barnard Spaull, former Chairman of WCSS. In a white jacket is Alderman Frank Kenton, the Chairman of the Ashmount Appeal Committee. Behind him is Joseph Sayers, Secretary of WADCOSS. The lady with glasses is Mrs Harriet Peryer, the Independent councillor for Offington, who was a leading light in WADCOSS for over twenty years.

point one of the invited guests presented a cheque for £1,000.[48] The response from the people of Worthing had been impressive, with £33,000 being raised in a little over a year. The new home would provide accommodation for 34 residents, although there were already 300 people on the waiting list – a clear indication of the great need that existed in the town.

In 1965, Mrs Florrie Frazer left a property – Little Court, on West Parade – to WADCOSS. However, it was judged to be unsuitable as a residential home. The property was sold for £10,000 and the money put towards the cost of purchasing Pulborough House, next door to Caer Gwent in Wykeham Road.[49] After refurbishment it was renamed as 'Frazer Lodge' and opened as WADCOSS' fourth residential home. The following year, WADCOSS received an anonymous donation of £20,000, not even the members of the executive committee knowing the identity of the donor.[50] This gift was used to purchase Dolphin Court, which was opened as flatlets for the more mobile elderly. Three years later, William Sloss left a legacy that enabled an extension to be built on to Dolphin Court, providing fifteen more flatlets.

As well as providing residential homes for the older residents of Worthing, Effie Methold had long harboured an ambition of opening an Old People's Centre in the town, with satellite centres operating in the suburbs. During the war years a site was identified in Market Street, but nothing came of it. Then in 1953 a planning application to convert 8 Ambrose Place into a day centre for old people was turned down by Worthing Town Council. In the meantime, WCSS was able to open, in 1946, a Darby and Joan Club in a temporary room at the British Legion, moving to more permanent accommodation at the British Red Cross Headquarters in Farncombe Road in 1950.[51]

By 1953, three other Darby and Joan Clubs had been established, and were meeting weekly at – Christchurch Hall in Portland Road, the Free Church Hall in Durrington, and the Parish Room at Broadwater. Although WCSS was very pleased with these developments, the annual report for that year stated quite clearly that, 'What is wanted is an Old People's Centre in the centre of the town which can open daily.'[52]

A robbery at the WCSS offices in Chapel Road in February 1956, during which thieves broke into the office safe, may have further concentrated minds on the need to find new and more secure offices.[53] Later that same year, Mrs Methold identified 9 North Street as not only a potential new office, but also the long searched-for social centre for older people. In the annual report for 1956, Mrs Methold wrote, 'Here, at long last, the twelve-year dreams and stirrings of this Council will be realised.'[54] Tragically, she would not live to see that realisation.

An outing of Worthing's first Darby and Joan Club in the late 1940s. Due to shorter life expectancy amongst men there are no 'Darbys' in the picture.

Ignoring all requests to ease up on her workload, Mrs Methold became increasingly poorly and was admitted to hospital in late 1956, where cancer of the spine was diagnosed. WCSS was forced to appoint a new paid secretary, Joseph Sayers, and gave Mrs Methold the title of Honorary General Secretary. Yet she remained diligent from her hospital bed, still reading correspondence and taking an interest in the progress of transforming 9 North Street into WCSS' new office and old persons' centre. Her death, at the age of 53, was a terrible blow to WCSS and affected all its members and supporters tremendously. It was little surprise that the Executive Committee decided that the new building should be known as 'Methold House', in recognition that, 'This Council and the town owe Mrs Methold a lasting debt.'[55]

Although the offices and the new centre were up and running by the autumn of 1957, the official opening ceremony took place on 5 July 1958, and was performed by Wilfred and Mabel Pickles, very well known and popular TV personalities of the day, most famous for their game show, 'Have a Go'. It was a day that attracted large crowds to Methold House and one that proved a happy day of celebration, fixing Methold House and the work of WADCOSS firmly in the hearts and minds of local people.

Wilfred and Mabel Pickles open the first Methold House at 9 North Street in 1958.

By 1959, the Methold House day centre had 300 members, of whom 39 were men,[56] an indication of the longer life expectancy of women. A canteen was run entirely by volunteers from local women's organisations in the town, without whom WADCOSS would not have been able to provide such a vital facility. Over the years, new activities and entertainments were provided, the variety of possibilities being greatly expanded when WADCOSS took possession of its first mini-bus in 1967. Right from its inception, it was intended that the members of the centre and of the clubs should take the lead role in deciding what events and activities should take place and that they should not be 'passive recipients of that which others organise for them.'[57]

During the 1950s and 60s, WADCOSS fought a long battle to increase the number of geriatric hospital beds available in Worthing. As the elderly population rapidly increased, so did the demand for hospital admissions.

This increase was also due to increasing life expectancy and improved health care and therapies, which meant that diseases and illnesses that would have once proved fatal could now be cured or alleviated. What was needed was a large investment in the caring infrastructure in the town, in particular, more geriatric wards or even a geriatric hospital.

Those suffering with poor health but financially secure, were attracted to Worthing as a healthy town in which to retire; often they would employ a full-time house-keeper to look after them. Florence Whitefoot [b.1910] was taken on by such a couple after the war to look after them and live with them at their home in the town. She recalls that the wife suffered from ill-health and that the doctor, who had not expected her to 'live more than two years', suggested they move from their northern home to the south coast.

Every Easter the ladies who attended Methold House wore their Easter Bonnets. Joseph Sayers, Secretary of WADCOSS, stands to the right.

Despite the doctor's prediction, both husband and wife lived another 30 years, dying in their late eighties in 1976. Florence jokes that she must have looked after them too well! It should be noted that this 'elderly couple' were not yet 60 when they moved to Worthing in 1946, another clear indication of how the perception of age has changed in the intervening years.

WCSS sought to address this problem as best it could, while at the same time putting pressure on the Regional Health Authority and the government to do more. In 1952 the 'Night Sitting' service was established. This scheme provided assistance for the elderly sick, who had no relatives or friends who could look after them, and were unable to secure a hospital bed, to have a trained volunteer, or 'night-sitter', present with them between 8pm at night and 8am in the morning. These volunteers were not medical professionals and were there more to provide company and reassurance than nursing, but of course they could call on the emergency services during the night if required. It is an indication of how serious the situation was during these years that the number of sitting sessions rose from 172 in 1958 to 348 in 1961. At that time, it was estimated that an elderly person whose condition was deemed to be urgent had to wait nine months for a hospital bed.[58]

It was in 1957 that WCSS first presented the Regional Health Authority with a 'Memorial on the Aged Sick', calling for the immediate creation of 200 additional geriatric hospital beds in the town.[59] The authority promised 50, but by 1959 even these had not been provided. Eventually a large geriatric provision was established at the former isolation hospital at Swandean, but it took many years of hard campaigning to achieve. The town's MP, Brigadier Otho Prior-Palmer, who took up the cause in the House of Commons, was the first to acknowledge the vital role that the Council of Social Service had played and that they had done 'a magnificent job for those pathetic older people in my constituency'.[60]

After 1971, and the creation of West Sussex County Council Social Services, the role of Worthing and District Council of Social Services was bound to change. Social work, which in the 1930s had been an almost entirely voluntary effort, had become far more professional by the 1970s, and this trend would continue and deepen, leaving a doubt over the future role of Councils of Social Service. Volunteer visitors who had undertaken small tasks for elderly people, such as collecting their pension, were increasingly marginalised by the new professionals who operated on the basis of legislation rather than 'neighbourliness'. In 1979, and with much reluctance, Worthing and District Council of Social Service renamed itself Worthing and District Council for Voluntary Service. In fact the name, 'Worthing Guild of Social Service' had been suggested as a more appropriate name in 1948,[61] but rejected by the Executive Committee at that time. In 1995 the organisation was incorporated, although still remaining a charity, and took on its current title of 'Guild Care'.

The homes have become more specialised since then, providing the high standards of nursing care when required. In 2002, Caer Gwent was only the second home in the country to be awarded the government's Charter Mark for excellence.[62] The home is now situated in Downview Road, having moved from its original site in Wykeham Road, via another property in Belsize Road. It is a brand new building with all modern facilities, which many of the first residents who moved in described as an hotel.[63]

In 1975, the Guild opened another new home, Irene House in Parkfield Road, Tarring. This was made possible by the generosity of yet another benefactor, Mr T.S. Gowland, whose only stipulation was that the new home should be named after his late wife, Irene. Mr Gowland himself later became a resident of the home.[64] Kay McLoughlin [b.1916] recalls how Frank

No longer arrayed with a flashing light, though still emblazoned with the word 'ambulance', the new WADCOSS minibus stands outside Methold House in 1976.

89

A television is installed in the communal lounge at Caer Gwent. During the 1970s, Frank Cave resisted calls for televisions to be placed in each of the resident's bedrooms at Irene House.

Cave was very much opposed to a proposal to put a television in every residents' bedroom, as he believed this would undermine the community atmosphere of the home, with residents staying in their bedrooms rather than coming together in the communal lounge. It was, she recalls, a battle that Frank persisted in for a very long time. Kay also remembers that some of the senior figures in the Guild, reflecting the religious origin of the organisation, objected to bingo being played in the homes as it was a form of gambling. Two homes – Whitcomb House and Frazer Lodge – closed, as they were no longer thought suitable to the modern standards expected of care homes.

Methold House went from strength to strength, taking over 7 North Street in 1960 and then no.5 in 1967, allowing for an increase in staff and users. In 1975 a brand new, purpose-built Methold House was opened which, with later additions, is the same building that stands there today. Sadly, Sir Arthur Linfield, who was knighted shortly before his death, did not live to see the opening, but Frank Cave, who became the new President of the Guild, did, and remained active until his death in 1992.

The Earl of March cuts the ribbon to officially open the new Methold House in 1975. WADCOSS Life President, Frank Cave, looks on.

The Darby and Joan Clubs, now known as retirement clubs, have evolved with the years, reflecting the increasing aspirations of older residents. Some clubs have closed, including those at Broadwater, Rustington and, most recently, Durrington. Older people with more money and better health are less inclined to commit themselves to a weekly club, with holidays, visits to friends, hobbies and leisure activities taking precedence. As well as Methold House, a thriving club is run at the Lovett Day Centre in Maybridge. Here the members tend to be much older and more infirm than the people who joined the first Darby and Joan Club in 1946. Whereas then there would have been few members older than 80, today there are few under that age.

One club that has flourished is the Ferring Retirement Club, founded by Lillian Holdsworth (Phillips as she then was), in 1980. Lillian was chairman of the Guild's Executive Committee and regarded as something of a human dynamo. Ron Duddy [b.1926] remembers her as, 'A highly intelligent woman with a wonderful personality;' while Frank Cave, writing in 1987, thought she was closer to the spirit of the founders of WCSS than anyone else working for the Guild at that time and that,

'She does not relax in her leadership of the Ferring Day Centre.'[65] Given that Ferring is said to have the oldest average age of any parish in the country, it is perhaps not surprising that a centre for retired folk would thrive in that village, but it still needed leadership and vision to succeed.

Methold House choir in the late 1970s or early 1980s. Florence Whitefoot can be seen in the front row, fifth from the left.

Lillian recalls how, with the help of the Guild's then General Secretary, Ken Spooner, she searched for a suitable venue for the Ferring venture and how she was prepared to offer an all year round service, including Christmas Day:

> There was no capacity at all in the Village Hall or the church centres, which left us with the Youth Centre. So we laughingly called ourselves the recycled youth club. But I opened that actually in October 1980 and Ken asked me to run it for a month or two until it settled down, and I was literally in charge of it for 19 years, and did every job possible, and for some years I used to open on Christmas Day and Boxing Day because I felt that that was the time when people who are on their own needed company. And I would take up my silver candlestick and things to make it a little bit special, and that was greatly appreciated. And I have to say those – looking back – they were really my best Christmases because I got more out of giving than I do sort of sitting indulging myself.

Like Mrs Methold, Mrs Phillips received no salary for her work, which was very much in the spirit of the voluntary ethos. However, the necessary changes taking place within the Guild in the 1990s were not always compatible with this thinking, and in 1994, the year the Rustington Club closed, the Ferring Retirement Club became independent of the Guild, and continues to thrive as such to the present day.

During the 1980s and 90s, Methold House expanded the activities available at weekends, including offering cream teas on Sunday afternoons. In 2003, the Healthy Living Centre opened, offering a wide range of services and activities aimed at ensuring the older users remained fit and active, both mentally and physically. A service was provided for those suffering from dementia and Alzheimer's, giving carers, usually a spouse or partner, respite from the demanding role of caring for people with this debilitating condition. This service is available two days a week. On the other five days, entertainment and other pursuits are available for any local resident over the age of 55. Of course, most users of Methold House are far older than 55, including Florence Whitefoot, referred to earlier in this chapter, who looked after a retired couple in Worthing for 30 years. Florence is approaching her 100th year but still attends Methold House. She has many interests, runs her own home and is a living testimony to the extraordinary improvements that have been made in the lives and expectations of older people in this town since the 1930s.

A careworker and resident at one of Guild Care's residential homes.

Three Teddy boys at the Mayor's Ball at the Pier Pavlion in the mid-1950s. Bob Spanswick (centre) caused a rumpus when he asked the Mayor's daughter for a dance. Rock and roll was banned in Worthing at that time, and the three lads were ejected by the police.

References

1 WCSS, Annual Report, 1933/34
2 WCSS, Annual Report, 1936/37
3 WCSS, Annual Report, 1936/37
4 WCSS, Annual Report, 1938/39
5 *Worthing Herald*, 8, March 1991
6 WADCOSS, Annual Report, 1961/62
7 *The Economist*, 9 May 2009
8 WCSS, Annual Report, 1952/53
9 WCSS, Annual Report, 1955/56
10 Cave, Frank, *50 Years of Caring* (WAGVS 1983)
11 *Worthing Gazette*, 13, April 1954
12 Quoted, *Worthing Herald*, 26 November 1965
13 *Worthing Herald*, 29 September 1963
14 *Worthing Gazette*, 24 April 1963
15 *Worthing Herald*, 3 December 1965
16 *Worthing Gazette*, 17 April 1963
17 Quoted from letter sent to the author by Mr Roger Sutton
18 Cave, ibid.
19 *The Times*, 7 May 1969
20 *Worthing Gazette*, 21 October 1970
21 WCSS, Annual Report, 1941/42
22 Cave, ibid.
23 WCSS, Personal Services Committee minute book, 17 January 1944
24 WCSS, Executive Committee minute book, 10 September 1945
25 Ibid. 22 May 1944
26 Ibid. 12 February 1945
27 WCSS, Old People's Home Committee, minute book, 24 February 1947
28 Ibid. 27 October 1947
29 Ibid. 23 June 1947
30 Ibid. 10 November 1947
31 Ibid. 8 March 1947
32 Ibid. 8 March 1948
33 Ibid. 7 October 1948
34 Ibid. 18 March 1949
35 Ibid. 11 August 1949
36 Ibid. 9 December 1949
37 Ibid. 20 October 1949
38 Ibid. 9 December 1949
39 Kellett, Edward, The Guild's First Residential Home (WAGVS, 1993)
40 *Worthing Herald*, 6 September 1963
41 *Worthing Herald*, 7 September 1973
42 Data supplied with thanks, by Julia Johnston, Information Manger, Guild Care.
43 WCSS, Annual Report, 1945/46
44 WCSS, Annual Report, 1952/53
45 WCSS, Annual Report, 1953/54
46 WADCOSS, Annual Report, 1958/59
47 WADCOSS, Annual Report, 1961/62
48 *Evening Argus* 13 June 1963
49 Cave, ibid.
50 Cave, ibid.
51 *Worthing Herald*, 2 June, 1950
52 WCSS, Annual Report, 1952/53
53 *Worthing Gazette*, 8 February 1956
54 WCSS, Annual Report, 1955/56
55 WCSS, Annual Report, 1956/57
56 *Worthing Herald*, 20 November 1959
57 WADCOSS, Annual Report, 1958/59
58 Ibid.
59 WCSS, Annual Report, 1956/57
60 Cave, ibid.
61 WCSS, Executive Committee, minute book, 8 November 1948
62 *Worthing Herald*, 26 September 2002
63 *Worthing Herald*, 24 April 2002
64 Cave, ibid.
65 Cave, ibid.

CHAPTER 5

Youth

'The number of children out of control and committing serious offences is steadily increasing,' so declared an article in the *Worthing Herald*.[1] The previous year, the Executive Committee of Worthing Council of Social Service (WCSS) had noted with concern that a 'recent incident' in Durrington had led to the closure of the local school, during which the children had 'run wild, become unruly, wore out their clothes, and did other damage'.[2] These quotations are not taken from recent reports, but from 1944 and 1943 respectively. Worthing has long been concerned about youth crime, although the level and the nature of that crime may have changed over the years.

This chapter will look at how WCSS, and later the Guild, sought to address the problems of youth in Worthing, a challenge that became increasingly difficult to address, given the organisation's growing commitment to deliver services for older people. As we saw in the last chapter, the town's growing elderly population in the middle years of the twentieth century created a unique situation in Worthing, which made it very difficult for WCSS to live up to its commitment to offer services to people of all ages and backgrounds.

Sussex Road School (now the Sidney Walter Centre) in the 1930s; the class teacher, Mr Fuhrmann, can be seen standing by the door to the left of the picture.

During the Great Depression, WCSS drew attention to the number of poorer women in Worthing who had to go out to work, often leaving children without adequate care. This, the council believed, was a consequence of husbands being unemployed or on low wages and the high level of rents in the town. It also observed that there was always work available for women in the service sector, either as maids in private homes or in the town's hotels. This led, as we shall see, to WCSS calling for the introduction of nursery school provision within the borough, which would allow women to work, while their children were under professional supervision. As it was, children were getting into trouble because their mothers had to work and this was leading to an increasing problem of juvenile crime.[3]

Gangs of boys used to meet and fight in Homefield Park. Pete Lock [b.1924] remembers these encounters, but also that the appearance of Mr Collins, the park-keeper, would soon bring these clashes to an end. Many of those interviewed for this book remember Mr Collins, in particular the fact that he only had one arm but also that he had absolute authority. Whatever the youths said or did to each other, they would not confront or attack Mr Collins, despite his disability. Interviewees all agreed that young people were in awe, even in fear of adults – something that will become very apparent, later in this chapter when discussing education. Phoebe Coombs [b.1923] recalls even the toughest lads being frightened of Mr Collins, and that all children at that time 'were controlled to a degree'.

Phoebe 'Pat' Coombs and her twin brother, Samuel, photographed outside their new council house home in Meredith Road in 1927.

This control certainly slipped during the war years, when the absence of fathers reduced parental authority, especially when so many mothers found themselves contending with the added burden of evacuees and having to join long queues for food and other basic essentials during these years of rationing. It is not surprising that under such conditions, children became wayward. Although those interviewed all professed themselves to be well-behaved children, closer questioning often revealed a somewhat different story.

Although no serious offences came to light, many people, who were children and youths during the war, remember indulging in petty crime. This included taking fruit and vegetables from farms and market gardens; entering derelict properties; breaking windows and

Revd David Burton, joint headmaster of Broadwater Manor School, walks along the seafront at Worthing in the late 1930s. By the towels under their arms, it looks as though the boys, conspicuous in their felt hats, had been swimming.

smashing roof slates; entering local cinemas by the back entrance, to avoid paying the admission fee; and repeatedly knocking on front doors and then running away. Perhaps Dorothy Ower's [b.1926] memory of high spirits amongst the children of Clapham and Patching in the 1930s is the most unusual:

> We used to go out when it was moonlight and we were quite small children and this was all before I was 12 years old, and we played out on [the Arundel Road – now the A.27], which is the main road. It wasn't much of a road then, but it was the main road for traffic coming right through to Portsmouth. I'd go out with these three boys and we'd make this enormous great big ball of snow and roll it right down that Arundel Road.

Dorothy could not remember if any of these giant snowballs ever collided with an on-coming vehicle – perhaps the children didn't wait to find out. However, taken as a whole, this activity, together with the others mentioned above, hardly amount to serious offences in a modern context, but they did worry people seventy years ago.

In 1940, the Revd Haviland, together with Mr Sidney Walter, proposed establishing a Youth Council in Worthing, which would work with all voluntary and statutory bodies in the town to establish 'fresh social amenities' for young people.[4] This initiative of the WCSS was readily supported by the Rotary Club, Worthing Town Council and the Board of Education. Indeed, the board later sent out a circular to all education authorities in the country, urging them to establish youth councils. Despite this ground-breaking initiative, Worthing and WCSS remained anxious about the youth of the town.

In 1941, Frank Cave warned that there was an 'appalling lack of knowledge' about juvenile delinquency, and that a greater insight was required than that currently being shown.[5] Later that year, it started to be reported that there was a concern that teenage children were being given too much pocket money and that this was leading to delinquency.[6] The Revd Haviland was concerned that older youths were earning too much money, sometimes amounting to more than that earned by the father, as a result of which the status between father and son had been blurred and the young man 'sometimes has more than he ought to spend'.[7] This theme was taken up in the WCSS annual report in 1941, which, while welcoming the improved social conditions of recent years, questioned the new-found affluence of the young:

> [it is] a matter of some disquiet that many parents allow their children to retain comparatively large sums of pocket money. Reference has been made already in the Juvenile Court to this very point and the Council from its own observations, and as a result of its very close and friendly contact with the Probation officers, supports the view that, to say no more, the giving of such substantial pocket-money to youngsters who cannot be expected to know the value of money, is unwise in some cases.[8]

This belief that children and young adults would be spoiled by having too much money at too young an age remained a recurring theme in WCSS minute books and in press reports into the post-war era. In 1947, WCSS established a Children's Welfare Sub-Committee to enquire into these and other issues concerning the younger generation.[9] Also in 1947, the Worthing Child Guidance Centre was opened at 6 Southey Road, offering the services of a psychiatrist, a psychologist, and a social worker.[10] These developments were all evidence of a growing consensus that children and young people had not been well-served by wartime conditions and that action needed to be taken to ensure that these problems were addressed and solved.

For the young people themselves, life had never been better; there was full employment and wages were higher than they had ever been before. Youngsters could expect to go straight from school and into employment, as Ann Miller [b.1939] remembers:

Boxing has often been regarded as an effective method of burning off teenage aggression. These two Broadwater Manor boys seem to be keeping their distance though.

You didn't have any problem getting a job. My mother had an interview with myself and with the headmistress and I think she fixed it up for me. I went to a solicitor's office as a general clerk. I was thrilled, I earned 30/- a week, I thought it was wonderful. . . . I remember saving up and buying a white jacket as my first purchase.

How different from the situation in the 1930s, when, as we saw in chapter 2, many young people were having to make do with cast-offs, and adult men were not taking home the wage that a school-leaver could earn two decades later. The affluent teenager had come to stay, but so had some familiar social problems. Young people with more money became more confident and less inclined to follow the ways of their parents. Cultural influences from America were also eroding the old hierarchies, encouraging young people to look elsewhere than churches, parents or traditional values for their sense of identity. Mary Martin [b.1934] remembers what a big impact this change had on her life and that of her friends:

Rock 'n' Roll came in in '53 – at the beginning of '53 when we used to go to the Assembly Hall. That was [the era of] Bill Hayley and the Comets. And up to then girls

Bob Spanswick with two female friends on the seafront at Worthing in the mid-1950s.

didn't wear trousers, didn't wear slacks, and we used to go in with our drainpipe trousers and winkle-picker shoes and high heels, and we got banned because we were marking the Assembly Hall floor. And Mr King, who used to be on the door, used to turn you back, as if to say, 'You're not coming in with those on.'. . . We used to have those winkle-picker shoes with those very thin high stiletto shoes. . . . And the shop I worked in then, it was like a little 'boutique' they'd call it now, but it had all the first rock'n'roll things coming in; they used to come from Brighton, and we used to do a terrific trade on them – it was well known. Every Saturday afternoon it used to be packed solid with them going to the dancing on a Saturday night, all wearing these three-tier skirts with net and tight waists. I used to dress the windows for them, it was good.

Worthing Town Council actually banned jiving and rock'n'roll dancing at the Assembly Hall and also, for a time, banned women from wearing 'slacks' at the dances. Eventually, of course, they had to back down because the new culture was far stronger and more determined to prevail than the old culture was able to resist it.

As well as exuberance, the new culture also had a violent side, particularly amongst young men who, less fearful of authority than their fathers had been, sought to provoke and goad that authority and assert their own ideas as to what constituted acceptable behaviour. Teddy boys frequently clashed with the police, as well as other gangs of youths. Alan Windeatt [b.1935] remembers that gangs used to fight each other on the derelict site where Hewitt's Fair had once stood, (now occupied by Marks and Spencer), and that these conflicts could be quite vicious with 'fists and boots' being freely used, although it was only later that gangs from Brighton came over, armed with knives. David O'Brien [b.1939] recalls that Worthing police would arrest groups of Teddy boys and then drive them up on to the downs and leave them there to make their own way home, having first taken the laces out of their boots!

This author has written extensively on the annual conflict that used to take place in Worthing on 5 November, between the police and the bonfire boys.[11] In those days the bonfire celebrations represented the old, traditional order, while the police represented the Victorian zeal for modernising reform. It is both curious and ironic then, that in the 1950s, Worthing should become notorious again for confrontations between youths and the police on 5 November. This time, however, the rowdy crowds of young people represented the new, American-inspired youth culture, while the police appeared as the defenders of a Victorian era, personified in the retired people who made up the majority of Worthing's councillors and aldermen.

The last serious disturbances on bonfire night in the Victorian era took place in 1887. Occasionally trouble did flare up in the following years and decades, most notably in 1929 when the police tried to prevent revellers letting off fireworks from the pier. On that occasion, the crowd, mainly made up of young people, reacted with hostility, and Marjorie Pressley [b.1916] recalls PC Dear being pushed into the sea. Bernard Poland [b.1915] remembers how the police arrested the main protagonist, Gordon Brown, and bundled him into a taxi; but the crowd followed them up the street, and, as the police pushed Brown into the taxi, the crowd opened the other door and pulled him out again. Later on an angry crowd whistled and hooted their disgust outside the police station.

Even in the 1950s, the old custom of people being on the streets, and particularly along the seafront, still prevailed. People, again mainly youths, built bonfires along the seafront from the Half Brick public house to opposite the café at Sea Lane, Goring. With the exception of 1929, these were good-natured events with the police keeping a discreet distance; but by 1956, the blending of an old tradition with the new culture of rock'n'roll and Teddy boys was creating a combustible mix. The proposed conversion of a youth centre in Portland Road into an old people's club in 1955 highlighted the difficulties faced by teenagers living in the town with the oldest population in the country.[12]

Increasing rowdiness on 5 November had been commented on by some people in the town, and Kenneth Wood [b.1938] remembers the game of cat and mouse that developed:

> . . . by the time we got into Chapel Road, up South Street, Chapel Road, you know, there'd be possibly over a 100 or more youths in it from any age from 12 upwards and we used to go up Chapel Road along Union Place maybe, along High Street and then the police would come out and try and break us up because we used to run – the police would come out and chase – we would run down the road, they would run down the High Street and up again and then we'd be going down. I remember we'd be going down

Bob Spanswick with friend, Eddie McBride. Shortly after these photographs were taken both young men, as a result of National Service, had to join the army.

*the High Street and the police came along Chatsworth Road to split you into two
groups. So once they'd split you up then they could split you up into even further
groups and by the time sort of, well, 10 o'clock at night, it was all gone, it was all over
because, I mean, in those days, 17, 18 year old, you would be home by 10 o'clock or
else, yes.*

It was not until bonfire night in 1956 that the first serious trouble occurred, as the
Worthing Herald reported:

*After the police had marched a youth away following a firework incident on the
Sea Front on Monday evening – Bonfire Night – crowds of Worthing teenagers
demonstrated through the centre of the town, yelling in unison, 'Let him go. Let him
go.' Traffic was unable to get past the throng which stretched from pavement to
pavement in Brighton-road and South-street and fireworks were tossed under cars as*

Prefects at St Andrew's
School in 1962. By this time
the Teddy boy 'quiff' hairstyle
had become mainstream, and
would soon be displaced by
the more outrageous long
hair style of the 1960s.

they came to a halt. At the Town Hall a group of youths hammered on the main door with their fists, shouting, 'We want the Mayor. We want justice.' The youth was taken to the police station but released almost immediately. He was not charged. . . .[13]

The following year, youths held a demonstration at the scene of the previous year's arrest. There then followed a stand-off with some officers outside the Assembly Hall, during which one constable was knocked over and kicked. When police cars arrived, fireworks were thrown at them, although the crowd soon dispersed.[14]

However, it was in 1958 that the most serious incidents took place. The week before 5 November, Superintendent Ronald Clapp of Worthing police had written to the Borough Youth Officer and to Head Teachers, asking them to persuade the young people to keep away from the town centre on 5 November. This plea appears to have made little impact on its intended recipients – indeed, the very attempt to stop people assembling may have inflamed the youth of the town.

David O'Brien [b.1939] was on the seafront that night when the rioting broke out. He recalls seeing a youth with a burning rocket caught under his coat, running across the promenade, although that was only a precursor of things to come:

I remember that quite vividly. I mean that was – I think if it happened today it would be called hell on earth. It was like a war zone. . . . I don't know how it got out of hand but there was fireworks going off all over the place – people were throwing fireworks, they were setting off rockets on the wall horizontally . . . there was a massive police presence, and whether they decided things were getting out of hand, they arrested a few, and 'course that started the trouble. And I remember the two that caused most of the trouble, one was a postman in later years; I don't know what happened to the other bloke, he was wearing a black leather glove on one hand and a black leather eye patch and they led everybody up. But it got worse, because they tore all the flowers up outside the Town Hall, smashed up the seats and ended up outside the police station, shouting.

Brian McCluskie [b.1935] was working for the *Worthing Herald* at the time and remembers his colleague getting caught in the thick of it:

The photographer from the Worthing Herald *had virtually the entire contents of the Town Hall flower beds thrown at him, because he was trying to take photographs. . . . The youngsters were going around with fireworks and they had got clay and they put the fireworks in the clay, stuck the clay on the windows of the shops and just lit the fireworks and blew the windows out. It was all very, you know, aggravated. The police . . . weren't going to stand for any nonsense and they were quite, you know, robust.*

This front page of the *Worthing Herald* is of interest, not only because of its coverage of the Bonfire Night riots, but also because of the news that the newspaper had won the coveted Newspaper Design Award – gained under Frank Cave's editorship.

WORTHING HERALD

No. 2010   FRIDAY, NOVEMBER 7, 1958   PRICE 4d.

ANNUAL AWARD FOR NEWSPAPER DESIGN

THE *Worthing Herald* has won the 1958 National Award for Newspaper Design in competition with a record entry of 286 morning, evening, Sunday and weekly newspapers throughout the United Kingdom.

This is the first time that the award—for the best designed newspaper in all of the three classes of the competition—has been made to a newspaper outside London.

Previous winners of the award are:

1954 THE TIMES
1955 THE SUNDAY TIMES
1956 THE OBSERVER
1957 THE OBSERVER

The award—a bronze plaque—and certificates for the winners and runners-up in the individual classes were being presented today (Friday) following a luncheon at the Savoy Hotel in London. The HERALD holds the plaque for a year and receives a certificate indicating that it has been chosen as the best designed newspaper. It has also won the class award for weekly papers.

THE PLAQUE

The plaque will be on display next week in the island window of Jordan and Cook Ltd., South-street.

The classes are for (1) newspapers published daily or on Sunday; (2) newspapers published each evening; (3) newspapers published weekly, bi-weekly or tri-weekly.

Newspapers eligible for the competition must have a general, not a specialised (e.g. literary, religious) news content and should be published in the United Kingdom.

Judging is made on a particular issue, chosen after publication: this year it was, for weekly newspapers, an issue of the week ended Saturday, July 26.

The judges for 1958 were: Beatrice Warde, of The Monotype Corporation Ltd., Vivian Ridler, University Press, Oxford, and Malcolm Muggeridge, former editor of *Punch*. There is a different panel of judges each year.

UNEQUALLED

T. R. Beckett Ltd. newspapers—the WORTHING HERALD, the SHOREHAM HERALD, the EASTBOURNE GAZETTE—have an unequalled record in the competition. In the first year, the SHOREHAM HERALD was judged the best weekly newspaper of 1954; in the following year the WORTHING HERALD was placed second in the class for weekly newspapers; and in 1956 the EASTBOURNE GAZETTE, in the same class, was highly commended. Only in 1957 was there no newspaper published by T. R. Beckett Ltd. in the list of awards.

In making the award this year, the judges describe the WORTHING HERALD as "a local paper

which achieved serenity without monotony, was neither overwound nor subdued, neither pretentious nor nervous."

They also say, "It is not a pseudo national daily; it is, in the highest sense of the words, a local paper."

The judges' comments in full and more information about the award will be found on page 11.

Here is the full list of awards for 1958:

Best designed newspaper of the year—WORTHING HERALD.

Dailies or Sundays— 1 *The Times*; 2 *Scotsman*; commended, *The Observer, Birmingham Post, Eastern Daily Press.*

Evenings— 1 *Oxford Mail*; 2 *The Star* (London); commended, *Evening Advertiser* (Swindon), *Belfast Telegraph.*

Weeklies—1 WORTHING HERALD; 2 *Middlesex Advertiser and County Gazette*; commended, *Harlow Citizen, Croydon Advertiser, Lowestoft Journal.*

November wet —and warm

Nearly half of November's normal rainfall has fallen in the first five days of the month. Since the 1st 1·60in. has been recorded, of which 1·28in. fell during the weekend.

The year's rainfall figure has reached 30·07in., compared with the annual average of 27·49in. November temperatures have been higher than usual. Monday recorded 59 degrees.

KILLED BY MINE IN CYPRUS

Worthing adjutant

ON a mountain road in Cyprus last Thursday, Major Edwin Alexander Andrews was killed when his vehicle exploded a terrorist mine. His driver was also killed.

Major Andrews, who was 39, was the son of the late Mr William A. Andrews, of Shaw-crescent, Sanderstead, and Mrs C. M. Andrews, who for five years after the death of her husband lived in Grove-road, Broadwater, where Major Andrews frequently spent his leaves, and who now lives in a Worthing hotel.

Brighton College boy, Major Andrews joined the Territorial Army in 1938 and served in the City of London Yeomanry ("Rough Riders"). He was commissioned in 1941 in 73 LAA Regiment, landing in Normandy on D-Day with No. 6 Beach Group.

IN PALESTINE

At the end of the war he was posted to a parachute battalion, being transferred in 1947 to an airborne anti-tank regiment, with which he served in Palestine as adjutant.

After service at Dover Castle and Coventry, in June last year he went to Cyprus as adjutant of 188 Radar and Searchlight Regiment.

Major Andrews was a keen fisherman and an excellent shot, and was an active member of the British Wild Life Society. He was unmarried.

The funeral took place with military honours at Waynes Keep Military Cemetery, Nicosia, on Saturday.

PIED PIPER

GARY MILLER, the former naval lieutenant who is now Britain's latest recording star, has been given the title role in this year's Connaught Theatre pantomime, *The Pied Piper*. See "Shows and People" on page 23.

SHOP FIRED—WINDOWS AND BOTTLES SMASHED

Bonfire Night damage worst yet

A CYCLE shop was set on fire during three hours of hooliganism in Worthing streets on Guy Fawkes night. Hordes of teenage youngsters wandered around smashing shop windows and milk bottles, and attacking police and others who tried to stop them on their free-for-all through the town. Even the police station and fire station were stoned.

Firemen tackle bonfire night blaze at Barker and Son's Railway - approach premises.

Judging by the damage done it was the worst bonfire night of recent years.

A firework stuffed into the letter-box is believed to have started the fire in the cycle shop—Barker's in Railway-approach—and others were thrown at cars and buses, into hotels on the Front and into pillar boxes.

Damage estimated at hundreds of pounds was caused as the crowds of rowdy youngsters wreaked their path of destruction from the Front, to Brighton-road, High-street, through Chapel-road to the railway station and back again.

Cars were damaged and a taxi proprietor who defended his cab by turning a hose on the youngsters was stoned and struck on the head with a piece of brick. Policemen were mauled, had their clothing torn and one had blood streaming down his face during an attack.

Police arrested a boy of 15, who is to appear before the juvenile court accused of assault on a policeman. No other prosecutions are pending, a police spokesman said. The worst incidents occurred when the mob moved into Railway - approach soon after 9 p.m.

Two 'yobs'

"I saw two 'yobs' coming in," Arthur Tavener, 47-year-old proprietor of Austin Hire Taxis, told a HERALD reporter, "and went out to see what was happening. I had several cars in the yard beside my house.

"I saw two boys coming in over the wall, one of them lit a firework and made to throw it at a car. I told him to clear out of it and he answered back using the filthiest language. He struck out at me and I hit him back—hard."

When more youths came forward into the yard, Mr Tavener got out the hose he uses for washing down his cars, and turned it on to them. Fireworks and stones were thrown at him

Teenagers and police in one of the frequent clashes.

from the crowd and a broken brick hit him on the side of the head, causing a cut and splashing his shirt with blood.

After some minutes, the crowd moved back towards Chapel-road. Fireworks and stones were still being thrown and when the police grabbed one culprit and marched him into the railway station, the crowd followed. Police closed the metal grid gates to keep them out.

Windows were broken in the railway station and the Victoria Hotel, opposite.

Fifteen minutes after Mr Tavener had gone indoors he heard shouts from passers-by that the store of an adjoining cycle shop—Barker and Sons—was on fire. He telephoned the fire brigade
Continued on page 4

FOR OUTINGS

A man using a wheelchair requires part-time services of a strong, young, educated person for outings and shopping. This is one of the small advertisements in the classified columns on pages 33 to 39 of this issue.

Burning your fingers

It's more easily done than you'd think, but there's no reason why it should happen to you. When you're faced with some matter of finance or business that takes you out of your depth, come and talk it over with us. You'll find us very knowledgeable (very willing to share our knowledge, too); and among our many services* there is sure to be something that will stand between you and digital conflagration.

Described in the booklet "Midland Bank Services for You", on request at all branches.

MIDLAND BANK LIMITED

2,170 branches in England and Wales

HEAD OFFICE: POULTRY, LONDON, E.C.2

Robin Baker [b.1943] was also in town that night:

I remember Bonfire Night in Worthing in the Teddy boy era. Obviously going down to the town to look at the fireworks on the beach, turning a corner round by Union Place with a friend of mine, and lo and behold, there was a riot going on – and just a huge crowd of a mixture of Teddy boys and girls as well – heading towards us. We just turned and ran. But what they were heading for was the police station, which they proceeded to throw fireworks at, all sorts of dustbin lids, stones. By then we just ran and ran and ran. . . .

Ruby Ross [b.1924] was married with children of her own in 1958, but she remembers that families would no longer go into town as they used to on Bonfire Night, for fear of 'the yobs', and that, 'You couldn't get down the town because they used to throw fireworks at you.' Pat Kerry [b.1940] was caught up in the melee and arrested, even though she had not been one of the rioters. She remembers how horrified her mother was when she received a telephone call from the police station, asking her to collect her daughter. Robin Baker was questioned by the police a few

Marine Parade in c.1960, a favourite haunt of youngsters on Bonfire Night. The Marine Hotel, to the left of the picture, was one of Worthing's original inns; its demolition in 1965 was much regretted in the town.

days later, when a sergeant and a constable called at his home. Even though he had not committed any offence, the mere fact of being questioned by the police so marked him as a young man, that even today he can remember their names and the serial numbers on their lapels.

In 1959, the town was teeming with police on Bonfire Night, many drafted in from neighbouring towns. It was in November that year that police raided three clubs popular with Worthing youths – the Capri, the Regency and the Granville, which were all situated on Marine Parade.[15] In all, 53 persons were arrested on the night of the 5th. Peter Dale [b.1941] recalls the Old Town Hall being used as a 'holding centre' for those detained that night. In 1960, youths, unable to mount any celebrations in Worthing town centre, made their way to the A24 at Findon, where they barricaded the road as a protest. Police reinforcements were sent to disperse them.[16] Mr S. Evenden, President of Worthing and District Chamber of Trades and Professions, praised the police for finally bringing the Bonfire Night menace to an end.[17] However, not everyone was so sanguine.

Worthing and District Council of Social Service (WADCOSS), in conjunction with the town's Youth Officer, Glynn Owen, organised a Youth Conference, and sent invitations to organisations across the country, the purpose being to harness the spirit of youth for good. In its annual report, WADCOSS stated:

> We were inundated with replies from all over the country, and the story the letters
> told proved that the younger generation is not anywhere near as bad as so many
> would have us believe. A scheme is now being planned in association with our Friendly
> Visitors' Panel for canalizing this desire by members of the various youth movements
> in the town.[18]

In 1962, Worthing schoolgirls were working as Saturday volunteers at Methold House;[19] three years later, Geoffrey Jordan, then joint chairman of WADCOSS, chaired a meeting for the setting up of a permanent youth organisation to undertake voluntary work in the town.[20] This fledgling movement was nurtured and encouraged by another leading light in WADCOSS, Mrs Harriet Peryer, the Independent councillor for Offington and one-time mayor of the town. Under Mrs Peryer's enthusiastic guidance, youth work in the town developed significantly, particularly directing its energies at helping the older residents. By the early 1970s, the Worthing Action Group, as it was then known, was: preparing meals at Methold House; decorating the exterior of Ashmount; decorating the flats of pensioners attending Methold House; undertaking shopping for the house-bound elderly and organising a Christmas Party at Methold House.[21]

Young WADCOSS volunteers take two disabled older people Christmas shopping in 1970.

Yet despite these outstanding examples of the young helping the old, some sections of the older community still felt that it was the young who were having too much done for them and that it was the young who failed to consider the feelings of the old. Worthing Townswomen's Guild called for the banning of portable transistor radios in the town centre,[22] and a suggestion in 1967 by Joseph Sayers, Secretary of WADCOSS, that the town should finance a group of cheerleaders to represent Worthing at the televised 'It's a Knockout' competition finals in Germany, received a frosty reception. Sayers commented that youth, who had been the butt of unsympathetic criticism, had been cooking 25–30 lunches at Methold House every Saturday. He added that, 'I am dealing daily with elderly people. I feel that an event such as this will offset the wrong impression that Worthing is only a town for the elderly and not the young people.'[23]

As well as the work of WADCOSS and the Youth Service, many young people at this time found companionship and a vibrant social life in the activities of the International Friendship League (IFL), which had been active in helping refugees to settle in Worthing, from the Basques in the 1930s to the Hungarians in the 1950s. The IFL also welcomed those from overseas studying or working in this country. Pat Kerry [b.1940] was a member:

In my teens I joined an international club when I was 16 or 17. It was a club where you met people from other countries. My friend and I met two guys from Ghana. They were only friends; they taught us rock'n'roll. One was going to be a solicitor and the other one was training to be an accountant or something to do with the law and we helped them with their English, befriended them you might say. . . .

The IFL used to meet in a room, reached up steep steps from Ann Street, but its success meant it was able to move to bigger and better premises, as Shirley Hare [b.1930], who was then General Secretary of the Worthing branch, recalls:

We met at the Adult Education Centre on a Tuesday evening once a week, and had a speaker . . . slides, discussion or sometimes. . . . I think it was a Thursday evening, we met at the youth centre in South Farm Road and we had a disco, and well, you know, dancing and entertainment there. And we got the older people coming to the adult education centre and the youngsters, mainly the international ones, coming to the youth centre that was very, very popular.

Members of the Worthing branch of the International Friendship League assembled in Richmond Road in c.1958. Shirley Hare (née Hayler) is standing, third from the left. The IFL was a popular organisation for young people of all ages, backgrounds and races at that time.

However, less popular with Joseph Sayers and WADCOSS were the coffee bars on Worthing's seafront. In 1961, Sayers described the coffee bars as being 'a positive precursor of immorality', in which young women wearing tight jeans and tight jumpers consorted all too readily with young men all too eager to take advantage of them. He pointed out that pregnancies amongst unmarried girls had been rising steadily in recent years.[24] Children born outside of marriage or to lone parents had risen from about 5% to 7% of births during this period, (in 2007 this had risen to 44% of births).[25] The sexual revolution was under way and Mr Sayers was doing his best to resist it, although not, it had to be said, with much success.

How different things had been in the 1930s. When two young people from Hove were spotted selling lavender in Worthing in 1936, they were referred to Mrs Methold, who ascertained that the couple, aged 18 and 19 were unmarried. She arranged for the payment of their train fare back to Hove, having first notified the Moral Welfare Worker in the town of their arrival, who, Mrs Methold was assured, would 'take a friendly interest in them'.[26] In 1937 it was reported that there were 40 unmarried mothers in Worthing who had to go out to work to support their children.[27] Today that figure must be counted in hundreds, if not in thousands. The Council of Social Service tried to support these women, both in providing funding for school uniforms for those children lucky enough to secure a place at a grammar school, and in campaigning, as we shall see, for nursery education.

This code of conduct, implicit and unwritten, was censorious not only of sexual misconduct, but also of relationships between people of different classes. Several of our interviewees told of their parents' dread that they should form a romantic attachment to someone not of their own class. One woman [b.1923] born into a

Left: A 1953 Coronation street party in Cheviot Road.

Right: Following the example of the Dutch anarchists in Amsterdam, Worthing Young Liberals introduced an orange bike scheme. These brightly painted bikes were left around the town for people to use free of charge. The scheme worked very well for some months, but eventually the bikes began to disappear, and the cost of replacement became prohibitive. But it was a lovely example of youthful 1960s idealism.

middle class family was told to end her relationship with her boyfriend as he was working class. Her father went so far as to lock her in a bedroom to ensure that she complied with his will. However, she climbed out of her bedroom window, shinned down the drainpipe and eloped with her young man – against whom her parents had no complaint except that he was not 'good enough' for her. This family owned a chain of shops, yet despite their wealth they would have been considered 'trade' by the professional middle class, who would not have looked favourably on one of their daughters marrying a son of theirs, any more than the 'trade' family had wanted their daughter to marry into the working class.

A Goring family enjoys a day out on Goring beach in 1939. From left to right, Faith, Eleanor, William (father), and Shirley Pakenham Beatty. Note the high breakwaters.

There was much hypocrisy associated with this apparent code of morals. For example, the businessman who jealously guarded the virtue of his daughter, might not be so concerned about the servant girl he seduced, or the severe consequences of her falling pregnant. Another female interviewee [b.1922] recalls how her cousin was seduced and made pregnant by the businessman who employed her. The baby was subsequently brought up by the interviewee's parents, only going to live with his 'aunt' at a later date. He was an old man before he learned of the facts surrounding his birth and upbringing.

Girls, particularly only daughters, were expected to look after their parents in old age, living in their house with them and not marrying. Even less encouraged was for daughters to follow careers or take up further and higher education. Many times, female interviewees have told of brothers who were encouraged in both education and work, while they were expected to become wives, or housekeepers for their parents. Violet Howard [b.1910] was not impressed with this choice as a young woman living in Worthing in the 1930s. When interviewed in 1999, she recalled the pressure exerted on her to conform, and her determination to leave home and take up a career in nursing:

> Well, it was father. He wanted me to wait on him. Mother wanted me to wait on her, and he said if I left home he'd jump in the sea or something. I said, 'Well, you'll have to swim, that's all.' Those were the days when girls weren't allowed out to do anything.

This strict moral code was probably more severely adhered to in the inter-war years than in the Victorian period, although it was rudely shattered during the war years. Writing in 1952, the authors of *Family Life Report*, produced in Worthing for the

National Council of Social Service, concluded that illegitimacy was not the stigma it had once been, due to 'the lax morals during the war'.[28] The report considered the problems caused by wives falling pregnant by other men while their husbands were serving overseas. Many babies born in Worthing during the war years had been fathered by Canadian and American soldiers who had been stationed in the town during the war. One female interviewee [b.1939] remembers her sister becoming pregnant this way. The father, a Canadian, was there for the birth, but returned home to Canada when his son was three months old. Despite him offering to pay her fare, the mother chose to stay in England.

The *Family Life Report* stated that the illegitimate child often led to marriage breakdown as the child was a constant reminder to the husband of his wife's infidelity. However, the report went on to say that many husbands had 'overlooked' the 'wife's lapse' and treated the child as their own, even adopting the child, which the report believed was a course 'felt to be well justified'. The report panel included Mrs Methold and Mr Elphick, the town's Probation Officer.

It was recognised that sexual ignorance was a major cause of unwanted pregnancies, and in 1946, WCSS called for sex education in Worthing schools, which would prepare young people for marriage by giving them spiritual as well as practical advice.[29] Sex was not on the mind of most young people at this time, which must

Broadwater Manor School boys on the shingle beach near Splash Point. The flint wall and tower seen behind the beach huts were demolished in 1939 and replaced with the present raised walkway and towers.

seem surprising and perhaps unbelievable to the younger reader. Joan Quarry [b.1927] was not prepared for her unwanted encounter with a Canadian soldier:

> *Although I was only 14, I walked or cycled in the town at night and mother never bothered that I was doing so. You didn't bother, and full of troops it was. I did have a Canadian once – asked could he walk me home as the last bus had gone. And I thought, 'Oh, yes, lovely, and of course he pulled me into an alleyway and said would I like to go a bit further. I was frightened to death. I was only 14. You see, I didn't realise. We didn't realise . . . we didn't realise they were sex starved, and he seemed nice. Fourteen I was. I went running home. I didn't tell my parents. Well, there was nothing they could have done. But that was the only occasion when anything like that happened. They'd walk us home from dances, kiss us goodnight at the gate – I had to be in by 10. The clock used to strike and then I had to go.*

Phoebe Coombs [b.1923] was just as naïve, and remained so until she joined the Women's Auxiliary Air Force (WAAF) during the war:

> *You would always see nurses with their bags and all us children thought that the baby was in that. Do you know we were so green – never mentioned sex! I went into the WAAFs at 18 and I was . . . in the MT section, there was men there and WAAFs and one of the girls said, 'Here,' she said, 'do you know that girl's been posted to another camp?' I said, 'She hasn't been here long,' I said , 'Do you mean that nice looking girl?' She said, 'Yes,' so I said, 'Why is she posted?' She said, 'She was in bed with another girl,' so I said, 'I sleep with my sister, what are you going on about?' Fancy, at 18, not knowing anything. There was a girl there, I thought she was old, she was 26 and she said, 'I've got a book you can read, Pat.' She had been a rep. actress somewhere and she let me read [her] book. That was my knowledge of what was going on. There was no sex education whatsoever. But you knew right from wrong. You didn't have to be told, you knew what you should do.*

This lack of sexual awareness was not confined to girls, as was demonstrated time and again by the comments of the male interviewees. Michael Luck [b.1934] spoke for many of his generation, growing up in Worthing just after the war:

> *Well, we used to go to camp fires at Bramber. We used to cycle up there to a Girl Guide camp fire. Some of the girls came from Moulsecoomb, Brighton and we cycled back to Moulsecoomb at 1 o'clock in the morning. Then cycled back home, then we cycled to Brighton the next day and met them at the under-cliff walk. I remember that clearly, about four or six of us. We would think nothing of doing that. It's quite a long way.*

Is this picture for real? The shadow cast over the man on the left, suggests it probably is not a fake. This untitled, undated photograph comes from the collection at Worthing Museum, and appears to be from the late 1950s or early 1960s.

We had no fear of doing things like that. We weren't very old, we were under 18 when we were doing all this. We never got into trouble or anything. It's strange, there were no evil thoughts towards girls or anything like that. They were just friends and that's it. It may seem strange to people now, we never thought of sex or anything like that. I can't tell you why.

Like Phoebe, Michael only learned about sex when he was in the armed forces, having never heard it discussed before:

No nothing at all. It was never mentioned at all. This is the thing. It always puzzled me. My parents never mentioned it at all. Never mentioned sex, ever. When I went in the army I was 18. My father said to me, 'Don't get into trouble, keep your nose clean,' and I had no idea what he was talking about. And I was 18 then. You can imagine. It didn't occur to us. We had no interest in it at all. We were very innocent like that, we were. Until I went in the army and they gave you sex education. Blunt, straight out! No messing about. That's the army for you. We were going abroad you see. They really do tell you everything. Nothing at school or from our parents; my wife was the same; she had no education at all from her parents.

Although it may have been an age of innocence for many, there were those who did have sex before marriage, including young women who became pregnant. Many of these women did not wish to become mothers at a young age, nor endure the stigma that having an illegitimate child still entailed. There were also married couples who could not have children, but wished to adopt. In 1950, Mrs Methold was instrumental in setting up WCSS as an adoption society, in fact the only officially recognised society in West Sussex. Over the next 22 years, the society arranged the adoption of 346 babies. There were very strict guidelines to follow, ensuring that the mother really wanted to give up her baby and that all other solutions had been explored; and that potential adoptive parents were fully vetted and judged suitable. By 1960, there was an eighteen month waiting list for couples wishing to adopt.[30]

By 1966, the impact of the sexual revolution was becoming apparent, with a steep rise in the number of unwanted pregnancies. In Worthing Joseph Sayers believed that this was a 'problem for us all,' and that, 'There are half a million illegitimate children in England under the age of 16. This should be your concern and mine.' (In 2005 there were 3.1m children living with lone parents).[31] Although the number of children born outside of marriage continued to rise, those available for adoption dropped off dramatically. Whereas 35–40 babies were being adopted through the society in the early 1960s, by 1970 this had fallen to 12 and by 1972 to only five.[32] The reason for this could be found in the greater availability of contraception, especially the contraceptive pill, and the Abortion Act, which legalised abortions of foetuses of up to 28 weeks' gestation.

Although the Abortion Act was supposed to allow termination when there was a risk to the mother's physical or mental well-being, in 1972 there were over 156,000 abortions, which the WADCOSS annual report for 1972 said 'should give everyone food for thought'.[33] In 2007, there were 198,000 legal abortions performed in Britain. In the same year it was reported that there had been a 21% increase on the previous year in terminations performed on girls under 14.[34] It is striking that so many more unwanted pregnancies have taken place in the last forty years than in the forty years prior to that, despite easily available contraception and sex education in schools. It is

Miss Worthing, probably in the early 1960s, again from the Worthing Museum collection. She appears to be sitting by the fountain at the Lido.

hard not to conclude that something has gone very wrong with society in this regard since Joseph Sayers expressed his concerns in 1966. The Adoption Society ceased functioning on 31 December 1972 altogether, due to a lack of available babies for adoption, although in its last year alone, 147 childless couples approached WADCOSS hoping to adopt.[35]

Education was a very important issue for the Council of Social Service in its early years. Its particular aspirations during the Depression years included the promotion of nursery education and the provision of free school milk. As we have already seen, WCSS believed that so many married women were having to go out to work in the 1930s because rents were high and husbands were either unemployed or earning poor wages. Women could find work in the domestic and service sector; but who

The children at Christchurch School, just prior to its closure in 1940. They are holding up posters relating to wartime campaigns to avoid waste and save money.

would look after their children? Miss Riley, Headmistress of Sussex Road Girls' School, found that of 215 girls she spoke to, 68 had mothers who went out to work, and of these, 65 had children under the age of five.[36] Many of these mothers were forced to leave their children with neighbours or unqualified childminders. It was reported that one such childminder was looking after 17 children, despite having eight children of her own.[37]

Throughout this period, WCSS argued persistently for nursery classes being attached to infant schools, especially in the most deprived areas of town. However, there was resistance, even from within the council's own ranks. Councillor Mrs Greenfield, who sat on WCSS' Executive Committee, believed that the problem had been exaggerated, 'There are not so many women going out to work,' she was reported as saying, adding that, 'Of course any mother would be glad to have us take her children while she sits at home.'[38] Not many working mothers ever had the luxury to just 'sit at home', and the realisation that something needed to be done gradually made its impact on the Worthing Education Authority who, in 1941, agreed to set up some pilot classes. However, the decision was overruled by the Board of Education, who stated that the proposal was not warranted, given the greater priorities of the war effort.[39]

Frank Cave receives a cheque on behalf of WADCOSS from Peter Diprose and Jane Bowen of Elm Grove School, Christmas 1970.

WCSS organised a conference on nursery education in the town in 1944, calling for the setting up of nursery-infant schools in Worthing as soon as possible after the war.[40] The need was primarily educational, as children would benefit throughout their lives in beginning their educational career at three years of age, rather than five. Also in 1944, WCSS' *Homes of Tomorrow* report urged that new neighbourhoods built in the town should all include a nursery-infant school in their infrastructure.[41] Yet, despite this bold campaign, Worthing had to wait fifty years before its schools had their first nursery classes. Writing in 1983, Frank Cave observed that the arguments put forward in favour of nursery education had been 'one of the outstanding pieces of valuable work ventured upon by the Council of Social Service.'[42] The reality was that after the war, WCSS was too involved in other issues, especially those concerning the elderly, to continue its pioneering campaign for nursery education.

A more successful effort was the one pursued by WCSS in the 1930s for milk to be provided free of charge to 'necessitous' school children in the borough. Support was garnered from the Children's Care Society and the British Dental Association. So strongly did WCSS feel about the need, on health grounds, of this proposal being implemented that it sent a letter to Worthing Town Council, 'pleading' with them to take the action requested.[43] On this occasion, the campaign was successful, and free

Schoolchildren march from the Assembly Hall on Commonwealth Youth Sunday in 1959.

milk was provided to children from poorer families, with other children having milk supplied at a reduced rate. In 1940, the Coalition government created a national scheme that also included expectant mothers in the free milk entitlement. In 1946, the Labour government introduced free milk for all school children, regardless of background. This policy remained in place until 1968, when Harold Wilson's government withdrew free school milk from secondary schools, followed in 1971 by Mrs Thatcher's decision, as Education Secretary, to withdraw the free provision from primary schools as well.

Many of the interviewees recall the introduction of the school milk, although not all of them got it free at this time. Anthony Rowley [b.1939] remembers how the crates of milk were immersed in water, to warm them up during the winter. Phyllis Mills [b.1938] recalls that at her school the crates were put in front of the open fire to warm up the bottles, which occasionally got so hot that they boiled over! Those old enough to remember the little third-of-pint bottles will probably agree with Barbara Windeatt [b.1937] that it tasted better when cold. At her school, the milk was often frozen when brought to the desks, with the cream having pushed off the bottle lids.

There is not the space in this present book to record the huge number of memories and recollections that our interviewees had about their school days. What is noticeable is that few felt they had a good education or that they learned very much. Even schools such as Worthing High or Sion Convent were described as being 'poor', 'not very good' or even as being 'rubbish'. Curiously, the happiest children seemed to have been at the 'poorer' schools, such as Sussex Road or Broadwater schools. Roger Davis [b.1929] remembers the basic facilities when he started school at Broadwater:

Mainly I remember we had slates the first year. That was 1934/5 I suppose. Yes, we had slates. I think we went over to pencil and paper about 1936, a year later in the new school. What I remember most was playing stoolball on the Green. It was one of the school sports, but it isn't played very much now, is it, except in the villages.

Ernie Blackman [b.1929] was happier when he was not at school, and remembers one day in particular:

I was off school and I used to be off school quite a bit with colds and other excuses and we had a school inspector used to come round – I used to live in Chester Avenue and he used to come round . . . and see if he could find any kids who were playing truant and I had to hide to keep out of the way and then when he had gone I went outside – and the street's deserted and it's a beautiful sunny day and I sit beneath the lamp post which was outside the door.

One reason some children did not like school was bullying. The other was the strict discipline then in force. Corporal punishment was freely used, with most interviewees reporting being caned, 'slippered' or hit with rulers or board rubbers. It seemed to be the policy at West Tarring Secondary Modern School for Boys after the war to find at least one boy to cane from the new intake on the first day of term every September.

Lower IV girls at Worthing
High School in 1957.

Saluting Headmaster Parritt? Actually boys at St Andrew's undergoing PT drill in 1950.

John Martin [b.1932] was caned for showing a boy a card trick on his first day, while Michael Luck [b.1934] was caned for arguing with other boys as to who should sit in the front row desks.

Yet no school had a more notorious reputation for caning its pupils than St Andrew's. So many interviewees have recalled the strict regime of the headmaster, Mr Parritt. For any younger reader wishing to understand how schooling has changed over the last fifty years, there could be no better introduction than to read the following reminiscences of Robin Baker [b.1943], who was a pupil at St Andrew's in the 1950s:

> When you changed classes it was a march down the hall, left side or right side, facing
> ahead and marching. I think there was marching everywhere – march into the hall –
> not as in soldier marching but smart and all in silence. Anybody that spoke would get a
> clip round the ear. When you look back it was quite violent really. The headmaster at
> St Andrew's was a Mr Parritt – he was a frightener. One day we were all called into the
> hall, the whole school, and Mr Parritt, the headmaster was on the stage with this
> young boy – his surname was Chamberlain, I remember the guy now and I often see
> him walking around – standing beside the headmaster. As I say, we were all marched
> into the hall. Then the headmaster, Mr Parritt explained why the whole school was at
> assembly, to watch this boy being punished because he answered Mr Parritt back. And
> the fashion he answered him back was that Mr Parritt said to him, 'Get into the hall
> now, boy,' and this lad said, 'Why?' Now that's the only answer back he said, but for
> that the whole school was marched into the hall whereupon Mr Parritt – I can picture
> him now – threw the boy off the stage and proceeded to jump on him with a bunch of
> canes. The whole school – it was like a wave – we all moved out of the way while this
> headmaster lashed out at this boy, across the back, the face, with a bunch of canes.
> And the rest of the teachers just stood behind and watched. It was the normal thing
> that went on. Looking back, it was horrendous.

The staff of St Andrew's
School in 1954. The notorious
headmaster, Mr Parritt, is
situated in the middle of the
front row. Derek Walker is
sitting in the back row,
second from the left.
Mrs Elphick is in the same
row, second from the right.

Robin was not the only person with such memories of Mr Parritt, although his were
the most vivid. For those who doubt the accuracy of schoolboy recollections, it is as
well to record here what a teacher at St Andrew's at that time recalls. Derek Walker
[b.1919] remembers his old boss very clearly:

> [He was] an old fashioned, loud mouthed man who only wanted discipline. As an
> example, I can remember one day when assembly occurred at 9 o'clock in the morning
> for prayers, all the boys were standing in the hall and he ranted and raved until
> 12 o'clock and when the staff got a bit annoyed about this and mumbled among
> themselves, he marched over and disciplined the staff . . . He loved the cane. He loved
> the cane. But we had speech days and sports days. I brought my wife to those do's and
> he thought she was very attractive and from then onwards I was well in.

It is one of the great fascinations of history and of human experience generally, that
while it is possible to find opinions that are almost universal, you can be sure there
will always be dissenters. So while the general opinion of Mr Parritt chimed with the
views expressed above, one interviewee, Cyril Shorten [b.1920], remembers his old
headmaster in a far more favourable light than many of his contemporaries:

> He was a marvellous master, he really was, beautiful handwriting, he only had one
> lung, he lost one in the war through gas, but, my word, he could shout and sing, he was
> a good music master . . . he was very strict, he wouldn't allow any nonsense of any
> description, but as I say he was a marvellous master, he really was and in spite of the
> fact that, you know, you got the cane if you kicked over the traces at all, but he was a
> very, very nice man indeed, I liked him. . . .

Perhaps it was Parritt's wartime experiences that for good or ill, fashioned the
personality so vividly recalled fifty to seventy years later by his former pupils.

References

1 *Worthing Herald*, 1 December 1944
2 WCSS, Executive Committee minute book, 12 April 1943
3 *Worthing Herald*, 26 January 1935
4 WCSS, Annual Report, 1939/40
5 *Worthing Herald*, 27 June 1941
6 *Worthing Herald*, 12 December 1941
7 *Worthing Gazette*, 17 December 1941
8 WCSS, Annual Report, 1940/41
9 WCSS, Annual Report, 1946/47
10 *Worthing Gazette*, 5 March 1947
11 Hare, Chris, *Worthing – a history, riot and respectability in a seaside resort* (Phillimore 2008), see Chapter.2
12 *Worthing Herald*, 11 February 1955
13 *Worthing Herald*, 9 November 1956
14 *Worthing Herald*, 8 November 1957
15 *Worthing Herald*, 27 November 1959
16 *Worthing Herald*, 11 November 1960
17 *Worthing Herald*, 13 November 1959
18 WADCOSS, Annual Report, 1960/61
19 *Worthing Gazette*, 3 October 1962
20 *Worthing Herald*, 15 January 1965
21 *Worthing Herald* – 3 March 1971, 13 March 1973, 30 March 1973, 6 April 1973
22 *Worthing Herald*, 13 April 1962
23 *Worthing Herald*, 9 June 1967
24 *Evening Argus* – 10 January 1961, 12 January 1961
25 BBC News, news.bbc.co.uk, 11 April 2007
26 WCSS, Annual Report, 1935/36
27 *Worthing Herald*, 31 July 1937
28 *Worthing Gazette*, 17 December 1952
29 *Worthing Gazette*, 27 March 1946
30 WADCOSS, Annual Report, 1959/60
31 *Worthing Herald*, 16 September 1966; Wikipedia, 'single parent'.
32 WADCOSS, Annual Report, 1972/73
33 Ibid.
34 Department of Health website – current.
35 WADCOSS, ibid.
36 WCSS, Personal Service Committee, minute book, 13 February 1937
37 *Worthing Herald*, 24 July 1937
38 *Worthing Gazette*, 22 December 1937
39 WCSS, Annual Report, 1941/42
40 WCSS, Annual Report, 1942/43
41 *Homes of Tomorrow* (Worthing Council of Social Service, 1944)
42 Cave, Frank, *Sixty Years of Caring* (Worthing Area Guild for Voluntary Service, 1983)
43 WCSS, Annual Report, 1939/40

13 North Street today houses Worthing Citizen's Advice Bureau, first established by WCSS in 1939. Mrs Methold was the first CAB organiser. At the time this photograph was taken, the house was the home of Worthing's first female physiotherapist, Joan Strange. Appropriately enough, Miss Strange was a great supporter of WCSS and its works.

CHAPTER 6

Health, Homes and Community

As has already been explained in previous chapters, Guild Care today is primarily concerned with providing services for older people and carers, but when the organisation came into existence in 1933 as the Worthing Council of Social Service (WCSS), its remit was much wider. In those days there was no Welfare State and no county council-run social services. The voluntary efforts of local charities, acting under the umbrella of WCSS, were the only means by which help could be provided for those experiencing hardship and deprivation. This chapter will look at the work done in the town to provide improved housing, free medical care and to strengthen the role of the family in the community.

Arguably the most influential document ever produced by WCSS was *Homes of Tomorrow*, published in 1944. This report set out the history of what today would be termed 'social housing' in the borough. More importantly, it included a survey of existing rented accommodation in the town centre, exposing the often wretched conditions in which many people were living. Finally, the report set out its proposals for change – a blueprint for the housing of the future.

Worthing's first council houses had been built after the First World War at Carnegie Road estate and were reserved for local people who had either fought in the war or were widows of those who had died in the conflict. Such restrictions would not be permissible today and it is no longer possible, in 2009, to reserve low-cost housing for locally-born people. Further council housing was built later in the 1920s at the Poor's Ten Acres in East Worthing, but the rate of building in no way kept pace with either the growth of the town's population or with the increase in depri-

WCSS ground-breaking *Homes of Tomorrow* report – copies were circulated across the country and even as far as the United States.

HOMES OF TOMORROW

A Report Issued by the Worthing Council of Social Service

Worthing's first council houses, built at Carnegie Road just after the First World War. These homes were reserved for Worthing people who had fought in the war, or the families of those killed in the fighting.

vation experienced during the Great Depression that followed the Wall Street Crash of 1929.

Between the wars the population of the town rose from 32,000 to 70,000.[1] The 1931 census revealed that nearly half the population of Worthing (49.6%) were owner-occupiers,[2] a significantly higher proportion than the national average. Despite the economic down-turn, Worthing continued to attract middle class professionals and the affluent retired. House-building reached a peak of 1,320 new homes completed in the borough during the financial year 1936–37.[3] Yet in the same year, WCSS was reporting on the lack of housing for poorer families and the high costs they were expected to bear. Too often, the cause of distress, it stated, were exorbitant rents, sometimes amounting to a quarter and in some cases as much as a half of family income.[4]

Michael Luck [b.1934] remembers well the hardship experienced by his own family in trying to meet household expenditure:

> *The wages then were only about £3 a week. That was what my father got as a builder/bricklayer. It worked out that you paid about a third of your income on rent and rates and a third would have gone for food and the other third would have been for clothing and things like that. There was no surplus for luxuries, nothing at all.*

One Worthing councillor accused some local landlords of 'grinding the faces of the poor'.[5] County court judges periodically condemned the high rents imposed on the defendants appearing before them.[6] Judge Archer, for example, asked how a woman charged with possession of stolen goods was supposed to pay her rent while also supporting herself and her two babies. He demanded to know if there was an organisation in Worthing that could help such an unfortunate individual.[7] It was stories such as this that convinced WCSS it needed to fully address the issue of poor housing in the town. It was in the latter days of the Second World War, when all minds were set on a new and better society, that volunteers from the Council of Social Service undertook an unprecedented survey of town-centre housing. Their findings would prove fundamental in shaping post-war housing provision, not only in Worthing but also further afield.

It is curious that the definition of a slum at this time included some of the very attributes that today would be considered highly marketable, including thatched roofs, low-beamed rooms, and diamond-paned windows.[8] *Homes of Tomorrow* reported that 88% of tenants interviewed had no bathrooms and that bathing took place in most cases in tin baths, filled from coppers in 49% of cases and by kettle in 14%; only 28% had gas boilers. Some people went to friends' or relatives' homes to bathe, while one old lady insisted she had never had a bath and never would have one! Ruby Peel [b.1927] remembers the tin bath hanging outside her home in Orme Road and also outside her grandparents' home. It was quite an ordinary arrangement for working class people at that time.

Dampness was a widespread problem, with open fires being the most frequent form of internal heating. Few homes had electric lighting or heating, and most people had only gas lamps or candles for lighting the upstairs rooms. Michael Luck [b.1934] recalls that during the winter, bricks would be heated up in the oven, then wrapped up in brown paper and placed inside the beds, to warm them up against the cold night air. Phoebe Coombs [b.1923] remembers waking up on winter mornings to find ice on the inside of her bedroom window. This was a very typical experience.

Homes of Tomorrow also revealed that 87% of homes had no internal toilets and that some tenants had to walk over 100 feet to an outside toilet, which may have been shared by more than one family. Only 48% of homes had a coal shed, which meant that fuel had to be stored indoors, along with bicycles and prams. On top of these problems, many people had to contend with infestation of vermin, usually mice, but sometimes rats. Doreen Ayling [b.1933] was living in a very old property in High Street when the survey for *Homes of Tomorrow* was carried out in 1944:

Stan Fishenden, with neighbour's baby and dog, stands proudly outside his new council house in Mendip Road, Durrington.

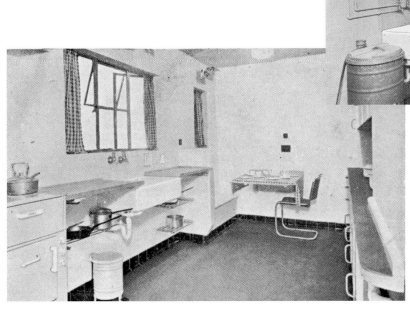

These two photographs from the *Homes of Tomorrow* report contrast a typical working class kitchen of the time, with one of the new, modern kitchens to be found in the council houses at Durrington.

As a youngster I didn't really know or comprehend if the roof leaked or the windows rattled but I do remember the noise at night of the mice running over the floor above us in the first bedroom, I suppose it could have been asbestos, could have been plaster, but we could hear the mice. There were showers of dust from the ceiling. Every day I would sweep up some of it.

Homes of Tomorrow called for the new council estates to address all the deficiencies in the existing rented housing stock. Its many recommendations included: full electric heating and lighting, including an adequate distribution of sockets; central heating radiators; modern kitchens with labour-saving devices; separate bedrooms for the parents and male and female children; ample cupboard provision; and communal gardens.[9] It was believed that the communal garden, maintained by the local council, would not only engender greater community spirit, it would also solve the problem, experienced in estates before the war, of gardens becoming neglected and overgrown. The estate at Durrington, completed just before the outbreak of war, included a communal recreation ground. However the omens there were not good – within a few years the young trees had been broken and the benches destroyed.[10]

Homes of Tomorrow gained a wide readership. Copies were distributed to all the town councillors, aldermen and chief officers. More impressively, copies were requested from across the country, as well as from the Dominions and the United States.[11] Only two years later, work had begun on Worthing's first new estate to follow the *Homes of Tomorrow* model – Maybridge. In all 2,500 new homes were built, greatly alleviating the poverty and squalor of the pre-war days. Yet not everyone rejoiced at the brave new world of municipal housing. 45% of respondents to the *Homes of Tomorrow* survey had stated that they did not want to move, some because they did not want to leave the town centre for estates on the edge of town, others because they saw their house – whatever its faults – as home. There was also 'an unmistakable feeling' that agreeing to become a council tenant would result in a 'lowering of class.'[12]

Newspaper reports from the 1950s and 60s, record a rising tide of dissatisfaction with Maybridge and the other big estates. These complaints included a feeling of isolation, the lack of local facilities and the cost of

The Strand shops at Maybridge, seen across fields. The Maybridge estate was the biggest post-war housing development in the borough.

shopping trips by bus into the town centre.[13] There was also a growing anxiety about youth crime and vandalism, which came to a head with the activities of the so-called 'Maybridge Gang' in the 1970s. To be fair to the authors of *Homes of Tomorrow*, WCSS had consistently called for estates to be fully integrated, with good local shops, schools and cheap and reliable transport links. WCSS also affirmed its belief in the central role of the community centre, an idea, as we shall see, that WCSS, and its successor, the Guild, repeatedly championed over many decades.

Whatever the short-comings of the new estates, none could doubt they provided vastly improved living conditions to those experienced by so many families in the 1930s, although the issue of private landlords over-charging tenants for cramped and poor quality accommodation did not go away. In 1962, Worthing CAB was reporting daily complaints from private tenants, who were being charged up to five guineas for

Raleigh Crescent, one of the last residential roads built at Maybridge, in 1957.

one furnished room, supplied by landlords, 'who squeeze an old double bed and an ancient gas stove into what was known as their spare room and euphemistically advertise [it] as a flatlet.'[14] Four years later properties were still being rented in which the only lighting in upstairs rooms and toilets was provided by candles.[15] Worst of all, one landlord was housing a family of six in just two rooms without any electricity.[16] At the same time, the slum properties of the pre-war years, those with low beams and diamond-paned windows were now becoming rather fashionable. There was disbelief in the town in 1963 when 39 Castle Road, 'a little old Sussex farm cottage', sold for £1,225.[17]

Not even Worthing Corporation was above reproach, and there was widespread concern when the council evicted two families from their homes in Maybridge just after Christmas in 1970. Particular attention was focused on the case of Mrs Molly Mustion and her two-year-old daughter Katherine, who were placed on the streets by council officials. Mrs Mustion's husband had left the home, leaving substantial rent arrears and the council refused to accept Mrs Mustion as the new tenant, instead describing her as a 'trespasser'. Joseph Sayers intervened, offering to pay her rent, but the council, in the shape of Mr Stone, the Housing Manager, would not relent. Despite the intervention of Councillor Godfrey on behalf of Mrs Mustion, Mr Stone remained unmoved and complained of the 'mawkish sentimentalism' of those who objected to his decision.[18]

In 1972 the Ugandan regime of Idi Amin expelled its Asian community, forcing many people to seek asylum in Britain. Worthing took in five families, some of whom had been previously expelled from Kenya.[19] The first family to be resettled in Worthing were Mrs Gulsham Jamal Kamani, her daughter, Shehnaz, and son, Shafique. Worthing Town Council provided them with a new home at 15 Newland Road, which WCSS had equipped and furnished during the preceding weeks. Mrs Jamal had been a social worker in Uganda, and the authorities there had seized all her property

Ugandan Asians welcomed to Worthing by the Mayor, Councillor A.E. Dunning, in 1972. Shown are Mrs Gulsham Jamal Kamani and her children, Shehnaz and Shafique.

and most of her money before allowing her to leave the country. On their arrival in Worthing they were greeted at the Town Hall by the mayor, Councillor Alfred Dunning.[20] Although the council provided the properties, it was WCSS that undertook the hard work of resettling the Asian families and turning the rather derelict houses into homes. It proved to be a 'mammoth task' but one that Sayers and his team had been happy to accept:

> *We are pleased that the Town Council had sufficient confidence in us to ask us to do this social and re-habilitive work, and when one now sees the happiness and relief of these families in our midst, and how they have been accepted by the community, it is a good reward.*[21]

Throughout its 76 years, the Guild has striven to address the problem of homelessness. In 1965, the TV documentary 'Cathy Come Home' shocked a nation that had been lulled into believing that homelessness was a thing of the past. The following year, Jeremy Sandford, the writer and director of the programme, addressed a packed Worthing Council of Social Service AGM. Yet it was not until 1989 that the Guild (WGVS) was able to muster both the support in the town and the finance required to open a hostel in Chesswood Road for homeless young men aged between 16 and 25.[22] Ron Duddy, Deputy Director of the Guild, was the driving force behind the project and the man generally credited with making the idea of the hostel a reality. The project soon became a victim of its own success. In 1991, Barbara Leighton, then Director of the Guild, explained their predicament: 'We are on average taking about seven referrals a month to our existing hostel which we just cannot accommodate. The need in the town is quite overwhelming.'[23]

The economic climate of the 1980s had created some very rich people, but the consequence of that shift in wealth was the emergence of a new cohort of homeless people, the like of which had not been seen since the years of the Great Depression. In 1994, the Guild decided that its expertise was not best directed to the very special needs of young homeless men, many of whom were battling with severe psychological problems, sometimes related to the misuse of drugs and alcohol, and the hostel was transferred to Stonham Housing Association, a specialist in this type of care. Other players had also entered the ring, including Worthing Borough Council, which opened 'The Foyer' in Shelley Road for young, homeless people.

Whitcomb House, renamed Delaney House in 2006 and transferred to Worthing Churches Homeless Project.

In 2006, Whitcomb House, Guild Care's residential home for older people in Selden Road was taken over by a charity, Worthing Churches Homeless Project, interested in the care of homeless people and recovering drug addicts, and renamed Delaney House. Pat Delaney had been a homeless drug user, who had been found dead in Liverpool Terrace; by the time of his death, his feet were in such a poor condition that he was scarcely able to move.[24] It is poignant that this tragic outcast should have ended his days in Liverpool Terrace, so close to WCSS's original 1930s offices.

Before the introduction of the National Health Service in 1948, many of the health care services in Worthing were delivered through the agency of WCSS. Frequently the Personal Service Committee would give grants to applicants seeking specialist medical advice or needing to undergo a period of convalescence. During the late 1930s, WCSS opened The Haven, a 'rest cottage' at Thakeham, where people requiring rest and recuperation could retreat for a few weeks from the cares of the world and find peace and relaxation. It was a most remarkable initiative and surely one that could prove very helpful in today's stressful times? A married couple acted as resident caretakers, providing food and other basic needs for their guests. One reporter from a local newspaper who visited The Haven was impressed by the tranquility of the setting: 'All around is the deep peace of the wooded Sussex countryside, hardly broken by the murmur of traffic on the road a little distance away.'[25]

Sadly, The Haven had to close in September 1938, when West Sussex County Council bought up the cottage and surrounding land in order to build a new school. The following summer a plot of land, close to the original cottage, was identified as being available for development. The plan was to construct a purpose-built rest cottage. Contracts were drawn up and an appeal fund launched, then, on 3 September, war broke out and the project had to be abandoned.[26] The following account from the WCSS archive is just one example of how the Personal Service Committee made a real and lasting difference to people's lives at this time:

An elderly man, who was in Worthing Hospital recovering from a serious operation, was recommended by the doctor to have convalescent treatment, as he was very weak and needing the necessary after-care. He was friendless and homeless. The Council [WCSS] was able to raise sufficient money to send him to a convalescent home for three weeks, after which time he returned to Worthing to see his doctor. Although greatly improved in health, he was still very weak and unable to work. Again sufficient money was raised to send him to The Haven for six weeks until he was passed by his

Worthing nurses during the
Second World War.

*doctor as fit for work, and he was taken back by a former employer. This
man says he can never express in words his gratitude for the kindness and
welcome he received while at The Haven.'*[27]

The Personal Service Committee of WCSS was able to provide what
were known as 'letters' of support for those needing medical treatment. These were in fact promises, on the part of individual subscribers, to pay for a particular aspect of medical care for a person on
low income; so one reads of 'ambulance letters' and 'surgical letters'.
Without these acts of goodwill on the part of local Worthing people,
much of the good work that WCSS was able to undertake in the pre-
war years would not have been possible.

By modern standards, much of the health care was very basic, especially for those
on lower incomes. Denis Spells [b.1931] remembers visiting Worthing Hospital at this
time and not being impressed:

*You went to the out patients up at the hospital – very small hospital and that was
pretty rugged, I think, ah, quite bad. All I can remember, we used to go in there – it was
all steel, you know, metal table, you know, put you on the table – steel and everything
around and there; all the tools, and I think they used to throw a bucket of water over
and wash it off [after] the previous [patient] and off you go and you'd be done, it was
that bad.*

Those expecting tender loving care might also be disappointed, as Teri Noice [b.1922]
discovered when she went to Worthing Clinic to have her tonsils removed:

*I had the tonsils out and that was quite an effort, that was, because they couldn't find
the – what was it? – the chloroform to put me out so they gave me gas. And I felt one
tonsil coming out 'cause they said, 'Quick she's coming round' – just got time to do it
and they cut this right hand one out and I felt it and of course I bled a lot afterwards
and we were all lying on stretchers in the clinic, and 'course I kept coughing and I
couldn't sleep for it kept bleeding and they came over, 'You naughty girl, go to sleep.
You are keeping all the others awake.'*

Joy Persich [b.1924], who was suffering with veruccas, was sent by her doctor to
Worthing Hospital for a course of X-Ray treatment. The result was that her feet
became terribly ulcerated. She was so badly affected by this treatment that she had to
abandon her ambition of becoming a nurse as she was no longer able to stand for
more than a short period of time. Even now, seventy years later, her feet are still

scarred and she has trouble walking longer distances. Today that doctor would have faced being struck-off or sued, but back in the 1930s, no one sought to question the opinion of a professional, least of all a doctor.

In 1932, the year before WCSS came into existence, the town was hit by a very severe outbreak of scarlet fever. So serious was the outbreak that all local schools were closed and, following two deaths, so was the hospital.[28] Those suspected of having contracted the illness were taken to the isolation hospital at Swandean, which had been established following the typhoid epidemic of 1893, which had claimed the lives of 200 people. Some parents insisted on keeping their children at home, in which case the authorities took extreme measures to ensure that the infection had been contained, as Derek Porter [b.1929] remembers:

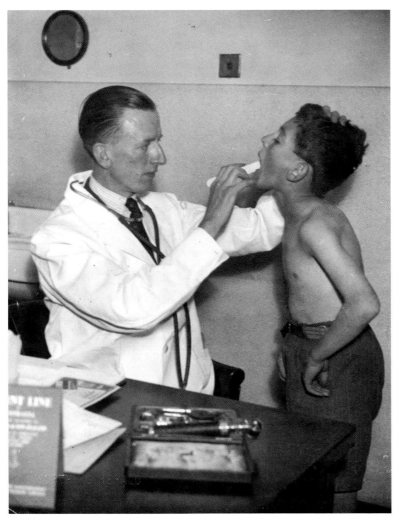

Roger Davies is given a medical examination in 1940, prior to a possible evacuation to Canada that never actually took place.

I should have gone to Swandean Isolation Hospital and didn't. They kept me [at home]. I can remember my toys were in the bedroom and after I was pronounced clear of the disease I was moved into another bedroom and I can remember as if it were yesterday, this green van pulling up outside of the property and two men getting out in a sort of brownie or buff coloured overalls things, you know . . . and they come and they closed and sealed all the windows. They lit this sort of huge candle – they closed the door and sealed all the way round and enclosed all my toys in there. I was devastated but we had to wait ten days and after ten days my mother promised me that I could go and open that door by cutting the tape around it. . . .

For those who did go to Swandean, which was the majority, the experience was not a happy one. For many children, some of them very young, it was their first experience away from home. Once in the wards at Swandean, they were only allowed to speak to their relatives through a closed window. Marjorie Pressley [b.1916] recalls that her mother waited outside in the freezing cold for so long that she actually suffered from frost bite. For up to six weeks these children were cut off from the outside world, having to make do with indifferent food and a robust care regime. When they returned home they were liable to be shunned by brothers, sisters and friends, who feared not just catching the disease, but also being sent to Swandean for six weeks!

The National Health Service, whatever its imperfections, was a massive step forward in the health care of the general population. In 1947, WCSS wound up its Dental Scheme, which had provided free or subsidised dentistry for adolescents and those on low incomes and transferred the scheme's remaining funds to the dental department at Worthing Hospital.[29] Many of the other pre-war programmes, run by WCSS, became redundant following the introduction of the Welfare State, including the 'boot' and free milk schemes.

By 1967, WCSS had become WADCOSS (Worthing and District Council of Social Service) and was preoccupied with developing caring services for the town's growing population of older residents (see chapter 4). However, it was at this time that the

Swandean Isolation Hospital, built in response to the typhoid epidemic of 1893, and still operating in the 1930s.

organisation's officers became key players in the campaign to open a hospice in the town for terminally ill patients. By February 1968, £1,000 had been raised for the 'St Barnabas' appeal, the name by which the hospice was to be known.[30] It was decided that all the money donated to WADCOSS through the Worthing Remembrance Fund would henceforth be given to the St Barnabas appeal.[31] It was anticipated that the hospice would cater for all terminally ill patients, including children and the elderly, and that their stays would typically span four to six weeks.[32]

Joseph Sayers, Secretary of WADCOSS, revealed that relatives of the terminally ill had begged him to find their loved ones better accommodation than the poor quality nursing homes in which the dying often ended their days. Dr Gusterson, for many years Honorary Medical Officer at the Caer Gwent residential home, expressed his dismay at the conditions which were to be found in many of the homes he had visited. He described so-called nursing homes where three terminally ill patients were cramped together in top floor attic bedrooms.[33] Sayers added that these homes were commercial undertakings, run for profit, but the hospice they proposed would be a non-profit making trust, dedicated to providing the very best treatment, given by properly trained staff. In 1973, the dedication of Sayers and Gusterson finally came to fruition when St Barnabas opened its doors at Durrington to its first patients.

St Barnabas Hospice as it looks today. Dr Gusterson and Joseph Sayers were two early advocates of the hospice movement in Worthing.

Serving the community has always been at the heart of The Guild/Worthing Council of Social Service's thinking. After the Second World War, WCSS set out its vision for post-war Worthing:

Some of the main problems of the next few years will be centred round housing and the family. After the long years of war it is imperative that family life be revived and preserved. The needs for full employment to ensure a livelihood and security has been recognised, but equally important is the need of some focal point, where the spirit of comradeship formed in the war years may be fostered – where recreational, educational, health and local government facilities are centred – in fact a building catering for all members of the family, from the youngest to the oldest.[34]

The creation of the Welfare State achieved some of these goals, and full employment remained an agreed political objective until the upheaval of the Thatcher years. However, the call for all-purpose community centres remained more elusive, as did the paramount objective of reviving and preserving family life. In 1958, WADCOSS, (as it became in that year), reiterated the need for community centres, declaring that, 'The development of community centres has become a more pressing need.'[35] It was not until 1966 that this aspiration was realised with the opening of the Sidney Walter

Students attending the Worthing College of Art and Design annex in Little High Street in 1970. The Sidney Walter Centre can be seen in the background.

Centre, named after one of the stalwarts of the Council of Social Service, who had also been a founder of Worthing Youth Council. The new community centre, right from the outset, sought to bring young and old together under one roof thus providing facilities for the whole community. Over the next twenty years, other community centres were opened in East Worthing and Durrington, although none of them, despite their success were able to provide the comprehensive services to which WCSS had aspired to in 1945.

In December 1952, a team of Worthing social workers, teachers, probation officers and clergy produced the *Family Life Report*, which was presented to the annual conference of the National Council of Social Service; its findings, therefore, were of interest to a national audience, not just a local one. Mrs Methold acted as the secretary to the working group. The findings were regarded as so important that the *Worthing Gazette* published large tracts verbatim, giving the report more

coverage than it did to either V.E. Day or the Coronation.[36] Unfortunately, the original report has not survived in the Guild Care archive, but the report in the *Gazette* is so comprehensive that it may be regarded as a reliable substitute.

The report's findings on illegitimacy and morality are referred to in Chapter 5 but in discussing this issue the authors also addressed the role of women in society. Many working class mothers were finding life increasingly stressful, and the return of husbands following the end of the war had not always eased that strain:

> *... she is often exhausted by her work and worries, and cannot give proper attention to her family or enjoy life, the home life therefore [becomes] unbalanced and unhappy. During the war years many mothers had to take responsibility for rearing their families for so long, and in many cases managed to do so successfully, that they experienced difficulty in re-adjusting themselves to their changed position when the father returned as head of the household.*

However, the report also asserted that the 'martinet' husband who did not regard his wife as his equal was 'now fortunately rare', and that drunkenness, once a significant social problem, and cause of marital discord, was declining. It was also stated that the increase in marital breakdown seen in earlier years was also declining, due to society settling down, 'unhindered by the upsets of war'. The report did, though, acknowledge that where couples where engaged in constant 'bickering', it was often better for them to part for the sake of the children.

A Worthing family wedding in 1946. WCSS was very concerned that family life should be restored after the disruption of the war years.

In 1946, WCSS, in response to the increase in divorces immediately after the end of the Second World War, sought to establish a Marriage Guidance Council in Worthing, but the effort appears to have foundered as a result of disagreements between members of the committee as to what the role and purpose of the new organisation should be. It was sixteen years before a further attempt was made to establish this service in Worthing, by which time marriage breakdown was once again increasing, with one in five marriages ending in divorce. The new service was established under the WADCOSS umbrella, with Lynn Wyatt being appointed the first Chairman of the Worthing Marriage Guidance Council in 1963.[37] Today nearly half of all marriages end in divorce, although, of course, far fewer couples get married in the first place. A reversal of this long term trend was observed in 2008, with the lowest number of divorces for 26 years being recorded.[38]

Several people interviewed for this project remembered their parents separating during or after the war years. In some instances, it was remembered that the husband/father was never mentioned or referred to again by the mother. Joan Bishop [b.1929] recalls that the one time her father did arrive at the family home following her parents' separation, he was drunk and abusive and tried to force his way into the house. She recalls that her brother forced him out of the home and that they never

Liberal councillors from Worthing and the surrounding district in 1980. It is noticeable how few are women, although the attitude encountered by Dorothy Till twenty years earlier had probably abated.

saw him again. Despite such a complete breakdown in the relationship, the couple remained married, for, as Joan explains, 'divorce was unheard of'.

Women, even in the immediate post-war years, whether they were wives or daughters, could still find that society expected them to follow the lead of fathers and husbands. Dorothy Till [b.1921] remembers that her husband was a great supporter of the Liberal Party in Worthing and served on the party's executive committee, representing Clifton Ward (now divided between present-day Central and Heene wards) although she voted Labour. This did not bother her husband, but it did bother the Frampton sisters, Liberal Party stalwarts, as Dorothy discovered when her husband became ill and could no longer attend the Worthing committee:

And the two Miss Framptons rang me up and said, 'Would you like to come representing Clifton Ward on to the Executive Committee until your husband gets better and you can keep him acquainted with what's going on?' So I said, 'Well, there's one difficulty,' and they said, 'Wouldn't you be able to get babysitters, dear?' So I said, 'That's not the difficulty – the difficulty is I'm Labour.' 'Labour! And your husband's Liberal!' So I said, 'Well, what's funny about that?' They said, 'Never heard of it – why aren't you Liberal like your husband?'

Several people, both men and women, recalled their parents imposing their wishes on them in terms of chosen careers, but this imposition tended to be far more resolute when it came to girls compared to boys, as Eileen Wright [b.1931] recalls:

Well, I always wanted to be a hairdresser. I had set my heart on [training to be] a hairdresser. And my dad said to me, 'No, you're not – you're going out to work, because you'll get all the grotty jobs, sweeping up and that sort of thing,' but in those days you had to do as your dad told you. Not like you can nowadays. You know, 'You're under my roof, you do as I tell you.' It was very strict and so that was very sad. And I wasn't allowed to go to any further ed. because we couldn't afford it and he said, 'You're going out to work.' There we are.

Joseph Sayers raised some eyebrows in 1962 when he appeared on an 'Any Questions' panel for Durrington and Salvington Townswomen's Guild. He was asked whom he thought made the best public servants, men or women, to which he replied:

Women are not equal with men. They do find it difficult to exercise their minds objectively, probably because they have children and have to bring them up, and that automatically makes them feel personally. And in a public debate they are inclined to take things as personally directed at them.[39]

The report said that Sayers' audience was amused by his comments, so perhaps his remarks were not meant to be taken seriously, but then again, 'many a true word spoken in jest!' One wonders what Mrs Methold would have had to say if she had been alive then? Nonetheless, Joe Sayers was the driving force behind establishing a Worthing branch of the Single Woman and Her Dependants. This national organisation was established to campaign for equal tax breaks for single women who looked after elderly relatives. Single men who fulfilled this role could claim tax relief, but single women could not. Dorothy Till [b.1921] remembers that Sayers persuaded her to become the secretary of the Worthing branch, even though she was married and had two children, but he believed she was the woman for the job, having seen how effectively she worked for other organisations in the town.

One of those other organisations that Dorothy Till worked for as a volunteer was the Worthing Family Planning Clinic, not a service everyone approved of in the 1950s. Dorothy was inspired to take up this work by the experience of her grand-mother. She also remembers how the age of the woman coming to the clinic got younger during the 1960s:

The Worthing branch of the Single Woman and her Dependants, though not all were women or single! From left to right, Miss Arnold, Miss Rawson, Mr Sayers, Miss White, and Mrs Till.

The Frankland Arms at Washington, c.1935, where 'Grandfather Golds' had been one of the last traditional singers in the district. The man on the right is Joe Rapley, a descendant of the notorious Rapley Gang of poachers and mill-smashers who operated in the weald of Sussex in the nineteenth century.

When you think my grandma had 13 children, and you don't mean to tell me you have 13 children by desire – no. So I got involved in family planning before you could say 'knife'. We were having a family planning clinic on Mondays. . . . We did begin to get girls. Quite difficult because if you knew somebody who came, you'd got to reassure them that everything you saw and heard at the clinic was confidential, otherwise they'd get worried, especially as I worked in a school by then.

The *Family Life Report* had noted that there had been a sharp decline in religious observance since the First World War, and that the grandparents of (1952) children had been the first generation not to give religious instruction to their children. The report also observed that some young children were taught to say 'grace', but this appeared to be more for show than out of religious conviction. It is to be wondered just how religious people were before the First World War, as even in the Victorian period only a third of Sussex people regularly attended divine worship,[40] although there is no doubt that the horrors of the First World War hastened the decline of religious beliefs.

Also in decline since the First World War, but not mentioned in the report, was the traditional Sussex culture – the Sussex dialect, folklore beliefs and traditional singing. Only one of the interviews that formed the research base of this project included a reference to traditional singing. Dorothy Blaylock [b.1913] recalled her Grandfather Golds would sing the old Sussex songs at the Frankland Arms at Washington. On one occasion two young Americans, captivated by his performance, sought to record some of his songs. Yet even by 1952 this tradition had died out in Worthing and only lingered amongst old people in the rural districts of Sussex.

Coronation Day, 1953, in Orme Road.

Worthing in 1952 was certainly a peaceful and orderly town on the whole, with crime rates falling throughout the early 1950s. A total of only 907 crimes were reported for the whole of 1952, most of them involving petty crime and theft and hardly any involving violence to the person.[41] During the first quarter of 2009, reported crimes averaged 633 per *month*, including 123 crimes of violence. There was also a monthly average of 533 'anti-social behaviour incidents' recorded.[42] The public's willingness to report crime, coupled with different recording methods, should be borne in mind when interpreting these statistics, yet the stark contrast between the two sets of figures is striking.

The press also reported in 1952 that a group of Germans staying in the town were attending a WEA course on politics and economics at Wilton Park near Steyning. Evidently the visitors were surprised to see men pushing prams and helping with the housework and were impressed with the orderly way in which the English formed queues at bus stops, as well as the resignation with which they 'put up with cold houses'.[43] One wonders what impressions foreign visitors form of modern Worthing?

It is tempting to see this period in history as a 'golden age', but as we saw in Chapter 5, the youth of the town rebelled with some vigour later in the decade against what they regarded as the stifling restrictions imposed on them by local authority. There was far less scope for individualism in 1952 than there is today and constraints of class, generation and gender remained pervasive. Golden ages may appear more golden at a distance than close-up.

References

1 *Homes of Tomorrow* (Worthing Council of Social Service, 1944)
2 *Worthing Herald*, 7 January 1933
3 *Homes of Tomorrow*, Ibid.
4 WCSS, Annual Report, 1937/38
5 *Worthing Herald*, 9 December 1933
6 *Worthing Gazette*, 5 January 1938
7 *Worthing Gazette*, 18 January 1939
8 *Worthing Gazette*, 14 November 1934
9 *Homes of Tomorrow*, ibid.
10 Ibid.
11 WCSS, Annual Report, 1944/45
12 *Homes of Tomorrow*, ibid.
13 Hare, Chris, *Worthing – A History, riot and respectability in a seaside town* (Phillimore 2008), pp.184–185
14 *Worthing Herald*, 16 November 1962
15 *Worthing Herald*, 4 February 1966
16 *Worthing Herald*, March 1967, cutting in Guild Care archive, no exact date given.
17 *Worthing Gazette*, 30 November 1963
18 *Evening Argus*, 5 January 1971/ *Worthing Gazette*, 6 January 1971
19 *Worthing Gazette*, 3 January 1973
20 *Evening Argus*, 6 January 1973
21 WADCOSS, Annual Report, 1972/73
22 *Worthing Herald*, 20 October 1989
23 *Evening Argus*, 3 March 1991
24 *Argus*, 13 February 2006
25 *Worthing Herald*, 14 August 1937
26 WCSS, Annual Report, 1938/39
27 WCSS, Annual Report, 1936/37
28 *Worthing Herald*, 16 April 1932
29 WCSS, Annual Report, 1946/47
30 *Worthing Gazette*, 28 February 1968
31 *Worthing Gazette*, 11 November 1970
32 *Worthing Herald*, 4 April 1969
33 *Evening Argus*, 16 May 1969
34 WCSS, Annual Report, 1944/45
35 WADCOSS, Annual Report, 1957/58
36 *Worthing Gazette*, 17 December 1952
37 *Worthing Gazette*, 1 May 1963
38 news.bbc.co.uk, 29 August 2008
39 *Worthing Herald*, 18 May 1962
40 Vickers, John, quoted in *An Historical Atlas of Sussex*, Ed. Kim Leslie and Brian Short (Phillimore 1999), pp.76–77.
41 *Worthing Gazette*, 14 January 1953
42 crimemapper.sussex.police.uk
43 *Worthing Gazette*, 17 December 1952

Elsie and Doris Waters ('Gert and Daisy' of stage and radio fame) open the Whitcomb House extension in 1967.

This history has been an attempt to reflect on the social changes that have taken place in Worthing since the 1930s. The method for doing this has been to draw on the archives of the Worthing Council of Social Service (now Guild Care) and augment these with the testimony of people who recalled how these changes impacted on their lives. I hope that I have succeeded in that aim. I would also like to think that I have succeeded in holding up a small mirror to the more general changes that have taken place in English society over the last 75 years.

Reading through all the oral history transcripts and the archival research notes, I was struck by the huge changes that have taken place within our society in the years since the days of the Great Depression. It is quite extraordinary to find people of 60 years of age or less being referred to in the 1930s as 'old', 'elderly' or 'bed-ridden'. It is no less startling to read of a soup kitchen operating in the town as recently as 1939, and that some poor people were 'too proud' to accept this charity. It all seems very alien and far away.

I was intrigued that the war, which brought with it so much death and suffering, also proved to be such a great social leveller. Unemployment virtually disappeared, while the standard of living for working class people rose appreciably – often as middle class fortunes declined. The war seems to have brought people together and softened class divisions. It was during the immediate post-war period that society seemed at most ease with itself, the 'golden age' referred to in Chapter 6, characterised by very low levels of crime and high levels of public participation in civic life. This was the era when up to 85% of the adult population voted in national elections, and when, locally, the Worthing Council of Social Service relied almost exclusively on volunteers to undertake a whole array of tasks and community activities.

Yet, as I suggested, such a reverie could be something of a delusion, or at least a one dimensional interpretation. How many of us would actually want to be living in 1950 Britain today? Would we not find it drab, conformist and unimaginative? Some readers may well answer with an emphatic 'No', and be only too pleased to swap our hyper-active, noisy, disrespectful age with

Mrs E. Baldwin, of the Old People's Centre at Methold House, collects halfpennies as part of WADCOSS' appeal for people to donate these coins before they ceased to be legal tender on 1 August 1969.

An attempt to raffle a car, donated to WADCOSS, fell foul of the laws then in existence concerning lotteries. Eventually the car had to be sold at auction, raising less money than would probably have been the case with a raffle or 'lottery'. This photograph shows volunteer ticket-sellers with the car, standing outside the old Methold House.

something far calmer and more dependable. But it would certainly not be the place for anyone with a lifestyle that even marginally strayed from clearly defined paths of socially acceptable behaviour; this, after all, was an era of stringent stage and film censorship and when homosexuality was still illegal.

I have found many of my beliefs and preconceptions challenged as I wrote this book, which is good experience for a middle aged man to go through. It was very apparent that something has been lost to our society, especially in terms of community and local feeling. The first council houses built in Worthing were only available to local people, while today's social housing is open to anyone who meets the criteria wherever they come from. Is this something to be welcomed or deplored? Does it enrich society by introducing new diverse elements into its social structure, or does it simply undermine the structure that already exists? I don't know the answer, but it is rather curious that the question is rarely discussed.

Olive Chaplow and her team of volunteer helpers outside WGVS' charity shop in Warwick Street in 1979.

I have been especially impressed by the great contribution that the Council of Social Service, now Guild Care, has made to the life of our town. I was first conscious of Guild Care's existence in 1996 while I was serving as a West Sussex county councillor. At that time I was involved in a campaign to keep open a county-run residential home for older people that was being threatened with closure. Fairfield in West Tarring was one of a number of residential homes closed by the council during the 1990s. Another Worthing home, Westholme, had been closed four years earlier. In response to this campaign, the county council was forced to reprieve Fairfield and sought to transfer the management of the home to Guild Care, as an alternative to keeping it under county council control.

The minutes of the Guild Care trustees for 1997 indicate that the county council may not have been wholly transparent in its dealings with the Guild. Indeed, at one point the Director of Social Services instructed the county treasurer to cease all payments owed to the organisation.[1] The minutes later reported allegations that county social workers had tried to persuade residents not to stay at Fairfield after it was taken over by Guild Care.[2] I remember those events all too well. It was not a happy time and caused me to question the motives and good faith of both politicians and officers.

The fight to keep these homes open had a surreal quality about it, in that the first closures were proposed by the Conservatives when they ran the council and opposed by the Liberal Democrats; while the second wave of closures were instigated by the Liberal Democrats after they took control and resisted by the Conservatives. The final closures followed the re-election of the Conservatives in 1997. Needless to say, such an experience did not enhance my respect for the political process.[3]

My faith in human nature, though rather bruised and battered over the years, has been immeasurably uplifted by the process of writing this book. All the founders of the Council of Social Service were impressive figures and all gave their time without seeking payment, or reward of any kind. Frank Cave received an MBE, as did Effie Methold, although in her case it hardly seemed sufficient. Mrs Methold was a tireless worker and a gifted organiser and yet she would not take a salary, nor court any publicity for herself. I was astonished that I could not find one photograph of her in the Guild Care archive. I was equally surprised how rarely her picture appeared in the local press, even though she was quoted in articles on an almost weekly basis. Clearly she avoided the photographer's lens and was content to be as anonymous as her role would allow.

Yet it would be very wrong to speak only in the past tense, for although present day Guild Care needs a professional staff in order to deliver its wide range of services, and to ensure the highest standard of delivery, the organisation is still very dependant on its volunteers. In concluding her annual report in 2008, Chief Executive, Antonia Bunnin, wrote:

> *One consistent theme throughout the year has been the commitment and dedication of Guild Care's many staff and volunteers. They are the backbone of the organisation, providing care and support for hundreds of vulnerable people, and I'd like to end by thanking them all.*[4]

Guild Care Chairman, Peter Robinson, trustee Derek Ridley and Chief Executive, Antonia Bunnin, congratulate Phyllis Bish, 104, on opening the new Guild Care charity shop in Rowlands Road in 2007.

The late Sir Philip Ward (right), then Lord Lieutenant of West Sussex, opens the Ashdown Youth Club for 10 to 14-year-olds in 2002.

In 2007 the Healthy Living Centre ran over 260 exercise and art and craft classes, none of which could have operated without the volunteer's time and assistance. The Guild has a fleet of minibuses, all driven by volunteers. Each minibus clocks up 5,000 miles a month, transporting an average of 1,100 people. Visits have included the Spinnaker Tower at Portsmouth, the London Eye, and the Sussex Diving and Helicopter Unit. Rather fittingly, each bus is named after a person who has made a contribution to the work of the organisation. The last bus to join the fleet was named 'Harry', after Harry Pressley, a former chairman of the old Executive Committee.

In praising the volunteers, the professionals should not be overlooked. Guild Care has a very impressive record in attaining the highest levels of professional achievement. Caer Gwent is the only home with nursing care in Worthing to receive the Commission for Social Care's coveted three star rating. Linfield has a special unit, the Richmond Suite, which has received national recognition for the innovative care it gives to people suffering from dementia. The Ashdown Club for children with special needs offers care and support to hundreds of children, young people and their families. In 2008, Ofsted declared that Ashdown had been either 'good' or 'outstanding' in its delivery of services.[5]

Service to celebrate
WADCOSS' golden jubilee at
Christchurch in 1973. From left
to right, the Mayor, Councillor
Harold Piggott, Her Grace
Lavinia, Duchess of Norfolk,
Revd Philip Walton, Frank Cave.

So, there is no reason to imagine the good work which commenced with that meeting at Heene Parish Rooms in 1933 has in any way diminished with time. In fact, I rather think that those early pioneers would be amazed and delighted that an organisation which began its existence with one desk, a few chairs and a borrowed typewriter, should have become such a centre of excellence, delivering services and providing levels of care that they could not have imagined all those years ago. It is good, I think, to dwell on achievements such as these, rather than regarding bankers and politicians as being the embodiment of the age.

References

1 It may be of interest to know that due to proven need, West Sussex County Council found it necessary in 2008 to embark on a programme of building new care homes in the county at a cost of £72m.

2 Guild Care Trustee minutes, 2 December 1996

3 Ibid. 7 April 1997

4 Guild Care, Annual Report, 2007/08

5 Ibid.

Her Majesty the Queen visits Methold House in 1999.

'The Donkeys and Marine Walk, Worthing', from a 1938 postcard showing Mrs Booth's ponies on Marine Parade, opposite New Street.

Indexes

Page numbers in italic refer to picture captions

Interviewees
with year of birth